Meeting the Challenges

stories from today's
classrooms

edited by maureen barbieri
and carol tateishi

D1530003

Heinemann
Portsmouth, NH

Heinemann
A division of Reed Elsevier Inc.
361 Hanover Street
Portsmouth, NH 03801-3912
Offices and agents throughout the world

We would like to thank those who have given their permission to include material in this book.

"Separation" from THE MOVING TARGET by W. S. Merwin. Copyright ©1963 by W. S. Merwin. Reprinted by permission.

Excerpts from "miss rosie" copyright © 1987 by Lucille Clifton. Reprinted from GOOD WOMAN: POEMS AND A MEMOIR 1969–1980, by Lucille Clifton, with the permission of BOA Editions, Ltd., 260 East Ave., Rochester, NY 14604.

Library of Congress Cataloging-in-Publication Data
Meeting the challenges in today's classrooms / edited by Maureen Barbieri and
  Carol Tateishi.
   p.   cm.
   Includes bibliographical references.
   ISBN 0-435-07225-0
    1. Language arts—United States. 2. Classroom management—United
States. 3. Classroom environment—United States. 4. Teacher-student relation-
ships—United States. I. Barbieri, Maureen. II. Tateishi, Carol.
   LB1576.M435   1966
   372.6'044—dc20   96-20397
                                                CIP

Editor: Toby Gordon
Production: Renée Le Verrier
Cover design: Barbara Werden
Cover photograph: Elizabeth Crews
Manufacturing: Louise Richardson

Printed in the United States of America on acid-free paper
99 98 97 96   EB   1 2 3 4 5 6

❋ *Contents*

 *Introduction*

Eighth graders tend to have lots of energy, some of it destructive: Patrick throws erasers at the chalkboard; Homer yells obscenities; Derek and Lenny have fistfights in the classroom. Younger children have their own troubles: First-grader Lee comes to school with a heavy heart, wondering when she will see her mother again. And Roberto, a student with Down's syndrome, and whose first language is Spanish, not English, struggles to find his place in a second-grade inclusion class. These students also bring many diverse strengths to school, but there is no question that there are times when obstacles to their learning seem overwhelming.

What exactly does "meeting the challenges" mean in the context of today's classrooms? Are the challenges teachers face today significantly different from those operating when we were in school ourselves? We think so.

Mutual interests and concerns brought us together around the theme of this book. For a year and a half, beginning in early 1993, we worked together on the Middle School Task Force for the Standards Project for English Language Arts (SPELA). That work widened our understanding of the complexities faced by so many who are teaching and learning language arts in schools today. The teachers we met were making language a rich part of their students' lives, yet they told us that although they were intrigued with journal articles describing current theory and practice, they did not recognize themselves, their students, or their teaching contexts in the literature. They were right. As we worked with other Task Force members to develop standards appropriate for a broad and varied population, it was difficult for us to collect telling vignettes that captured a national picture.

SPELA's work came to an early end in February of 1994, to be taken up by the National Council of Teachers of English (NCTE) and the International Reading Association (IRA). Our work together, however, had just begun. We decided to compile a book that would bring to light the attempts of strong teachers to reach all the students who fill their classrooms. Writers for our book would be teachers who recognize their students' strengths as well as their needs and who strive every day to find ways to build on these strengths. These would be teachers who rely on both traditional and innovative approaches to enliven and deepen understanding. These would be teachers whose stories cry out to be told, whose stories offer answers to the many questions we still pondered as SPELA disbanded:

- In what ways do we as language arts teachers value diversity, support home language, and respect multiple cultures in our classrooms?
- How do we balance our commitment to the entire group with our concern for the isolated, disinterested student?
- When children appear alienated, angry, and resistant, how do we enable them to be part of the classroom community?
- What can we learn from children who seem resistant? What is the nature of their resistance? Does resistance serve them in ways we need to understand and build on?
- How do we provide the fundamentals of good language arts instruction to all children?
- How are we coping with failures? Every teacher must face the heartbreak of not being able to reach a student. What do we learn from these students, and where do we go from here?

We cast our net wide, looking for teachers who shared our interest in these questions and whose own classroom research, observations of students, and daily experiences had led them to new understandings of their students and new insights about themselves as teachers. The writing we received also began to redefine the working title of the book, *Meeting the Challenges.* Teachers weren't writing about finding answers; they weren't sending us success stories; they weren't describing how-to techniques that would ensure every child's learning. Instead, they were writing about their own learning journeys—about what they were learning from students who were seen by others as apathetic, alienated, or resistant, or who were labeled as "students at risk" or "language deficient." They were writing about their own inner turmoil and self-questioning amidst difficult moments in the classroom. They were writing about small victories, tenuous progress, and the big and small rewards of really paying attention to who is in the classroom and then doing a good job of teaching those students. This, indeed, was the real picture of meeting the challenges in one's classroom.

While the authors you will meet here represent great diversity geographically, demographically, and even philosophically, they often share several common goals as teachers. They have high expectations for all students, and they are determined to pursue thoughtful, if varied, approaches to ensure success and achievement, whether that means bringing rocking chairs into the classroom, suggesting anonymous team journal writing, or encouraging video productions. They all have the compassion and the good sense to get to know their students as individuals—no easy feat in this era of huge classes—discovering disparate strengths and passions and then building on these. They believe that literacy can and will make a difference in the lives of their students; reading and writing are not just school subjects but endeavors that matter far beyond the classroom walls. Janine Chappell Carr's students in California, for example, discover that their grief is assuaged when they write about it or when they encounter characters in books who feel what they feel; Nick D'Alessandro's middle schoolers from Hell's Kitchen in New York pass notes in his class, working out the complex details of their social lives.

These teachers are creative, refusing to be locked into any dogmatic methodology, recognizing that because students are unique, each may need an adapted assignment or a different instructional technique. Because they are so well read themselves, these teachers know which book to suggest to whom and when to do it. Because they are also writers, they urge students, gently and not so gently, to get busy examining "the stuff of their lives" with their pens. They work to build in their students self-confidence, respect for others, and passionate curiosity about the world.

Without exception, the authors write of the absolute need of a community in the classroom—a shared sense of purpose; a commitment to the good of the group as each member pulls for the others; a sense that here students will be safe and their feelings, ideas, questions, and values will be respected. In these classroom communities, talk is valued most highly of all; children and adolescents have the chance to speak their minds while others in the room honor them by listening well. As we read these teachers' stories, we come to understand that their work has less to do with teaching language arts than with inviting students to use their learning to understand their lives.

Some teachers sent us poignant anecdotes about former students they cannot forget or about particularly challenging experiences that stay with them, even though years have passed. Others sent us poems. We believe these are equally provocative, and we present them here as interludes among the chapters, hoping readers will recognize their own challenges and relationships with young people.

As you read this book, you will hear the voices of eighteen classroom practitioners whose stories have helped us understand what good teaching can be. We hope that you will see aspects of yourselves here and that you will feel connected to the rich mosaic of diverse classrooms you discover. We also hope that these stories will inspire all teachers to remember that, in Maya Angelou's words, "All the children are our children." Whether we teach in East St. Louis, Illinois, in Santa Cruz, California, or in Scarsdale, New York, we are charged with promoting the literacy and learning of all students. How are we meeting the challenges, against all the odds our children face, in and beyond our own classrooms? We invite you to listen to the voices of caring, committed professionals and then ponder for yourself how you too might make a difference in this most challenging world.

Maureen Barbieri
Carol Tateishi

Can I Speak Gussak?
Using Literature
with a Special Education Class

Margo Ackerman

Oct. 7 Day 1

I want to quit. I have no idea how I will ever get through this. When Brian greeted me at home, I burst into tears and asked him if we had enough money for me to take a sabbatical. I've been crying off and on ever since. I can't stop.

These are the first words entered into a journal that was to chronical one year of my teaching life. That night's entry continued:

The classroom looks like a large abandoned closet. The "new" thermal windows are completely fogged up so that they are practically opaque. If we want to see out, we have to open them, and, with the exception of one, they only open about six inches. There are two closets that, even if they did open, I would have trouble getting my pocketbook into let alone twenty-some boxes of books and materials. There are about twelve desks with chairs attached, one ancient, green metal cabinet, one small dented bookcase, and a rectangular table who's top is partly removed. The walls are bare. After beginning to unpack what few materials I had in the room with me, Kathy, the assistant teacher for this group, filled me in on some of the "school business" stuff. We were just beginning to talk about how poorly this transition had been handled when the bell rang.

Within seconds, nine boys between the ages of twelve and fourteen came bounding into the room. The first words I heard were, "Hey you ain't staying the fuck here 'cause we're gonna make sure you don't," a comment that I was to hear in various forms throughout the day. The day went downhill from there. I assured them that I was staying but, my god, I really don't want to. There was chaos almost all day. Patrick threw erasers at the chalkboard, Reggie lit matches in the trash can, Homer kept yelling "fuck you, fuck this shit, this bitch ain't staying here" and was in and out of the room all day. There were at least two fistfights. Derek and Lenny went at it in class and Robert and Rasheed ended up in the hallway followed by the entire class. Trevor attempted to climb out of our third-story window three times. The third time I went over to him, put my hand on his leg that was still in the room, and told him that I would be very sad if he jumped out of the window—but the decision really was his to make. Then I walked away. That was the last time he attempted to leave via the window, as far as I know.

We did have quieter times. Sometime during the morning we had a math period. No teaching. Just me throwing dittos in front of them. The other time was at about 11:30. I grabbed *Sign of the Beaver* and gave a copy to the four kids who remained in the class, Derek, Rasheed, Patrick, and Robert. The rest of the class was gone. I don't know where they went. Kathy wrote up cut slips and I pretended that it was perfectly normal to have a class size of four children and two adults. We actually read, though! I arranged the desks in a circle and I read to them as they followed or just listened. Every time I looked up from my book, Rasheed and Derek were staring at me. They seemed to be listening. We read about three chapters (very quickly), and then the yelling and fighting and cursing began again.

I don't know how I made it to lunch and then Prep. I really can't remember. I don't know how I'm going to go back tomorrow. And the next day, and the next . . . I chose to come here. I chose to leave Sullivan. I feel like a fool, like a failure. I'm the teacher who can't control her kids. I'm the teacher whose kids are in the hall. These children are too much for me. I can't go back. ■

I have been a special education teacher in the Philadelphia Public School system for fifteen years, thirteen of them in an elementary school. During this time, I had developed a love for using literature with kids, giving children time to work cooperatively, and providing them with large blocks of time for reading and writing. But in my thirteenth year, I found myself thinking more and more about teaching older students. Because of my strong interest in literature, I was particularly excited about developing a curriculum around novels written for adolescents. In the spring of 1991, I put in a request to transfer to a middle or high school. In the first week of September, my transfer was approved. Almost everyone I knew advised me against making the move. Few people could imagine why I wanted to leave my secure position in an elementary school for a middle school. I made the move, but was not prepared for what followed. I arrived at Harding Middle School on October seventh of that year, a month into the new semester. This also meant that my new class lost a teacher that they had had for a month and were just beginning to know.

Harding is a school of about 1,100 students, grades six through eight. 65 percent are white, 30 percent are African American, and the Asian American and Latino population together comprise about 5 percent. The school neighborhood is a working-class community with a high rate of unemployment and underemployment. It is also racially mixed, with a predominance of African Americans and whites.

My new class was labeled an Emotional Support class. There were twelve students ages twelve to fourteen, and a full-time assistant teacher, Kathy. Four of the children had been previously hospitalized for psychiatric reasons, two had been in private schools for children with emotional problems (until the funding was stopped), and one child was spending his evenings at the Juvenile Detention Center. All of the students were male. Six of the boys were African American, five were white, and one was Latino.

A concern that had been a part of my teaching for many years was the issue of creating a sense of community in the classroom. The push in special education has been toward individualizing—individual educational plans, the use of homogeneous reading groups, and special education classes as separate individuals from the larger community. Yet the times when I feel most like a successful teacher are those times when I see kids helping each other, having a dynamic group discussion, or making references to something our class has discovered together. As I tried to define what "having a sense of community" means, I wondered: What do I do as a teacher to detract from or enhance a class' sense of community? How does the institution of a curriculum detract from or enhance the development of community? How do differences in race, class, and gender influence community?

After my first day at Harding, I wondered how we were going to survive the chaos and the violence of this class, let alone develop any semblance of community among us. I was devastated, yet I suspected not only that this was a class that would benefit from the development of community, but also that a sense of community was crucial if any learning was to happen at all.

I insisted from the first day that when we read, we were going to arrange our desks in a circle. Despite their balking and the surprisingly long time that it took to actually make a circle, I felt that this was a way for me to gather them together, to develop a closeness. It was a way for us to make eye contact, to feel like a group.

On the third day, there were six students in our reading circle. Each day our numbers were growing.

Oct. 9 Day 3

I did not cry on my way home from school today. On the radio was a song whose chorus was "and here we're starting over again. . . ." Today during *Sign of the Beaver* six kids were sitting in a circle and following, listening, and reading along. Derek, Robert, Rasheed, Patrick, Lenny, and Dean (although he was sleeping) formed the inner circle. Bobby was close by on the perimeter. Reggie sat at the edge of the room and made sounds while ejecting small pebbles from his homemade slingshot. Derek helped read in a kind of rap style. He loves when Attean (the Native American protagonist) refers to Matthew as "white boy." He demands that everyone listen as he repeats those lines. Derek and Rasheed seemed a little surprised that the book was using those words "white boy." And every time Derek brought attention to them, he looked at me. I think he expected me to stop him from making fun. I was thrilled that it caught their attention. We laughed while we read today. It felt so fragile, so tentative, but we laughed.

Then, after reading today, I set the glass jar with the caterpillar I brought in on the bookcase. It's been sitting in my book bag for almost three days now. I've been afraid to take it out while the kids are here. It seemed appropriate to bring it out now, while we were talking about nature and the forest in *Sign of the Beaver*. Derek noticed it and showed the others. We talked a lot about it. How it would change, where it would go, how it would get there. They asked questions and almost waited for the answers. You have to be really quick in this class. I also talked about the silkworms that I have in the 'fridge and that we'll have this spring. Again they asked me questions. It seemed that talking about what was going to happen down the line helped them to *almost* believe that I was going to stay. A short time after this Rasheed looked at me quizzically and said, "You really like it here don't you?" I answered, "Yes, Rasheed, I really like it here." Maybe Rasheed saw something in me that I did not. What I did see was that these kids desperately needed someone to *want* to be there.

The rest of the day is sort of a blur with Patrick jumping out of his seat every fourteen seconds to play basketball with the erasers (which I am not quick enough to hide), and Reggie muttering curses under his breath almost all day long, and Dean roaming around the room as if looking for and not finding a way out, and Rasheed repeatedly seeking out Bobby just so he could punch him before Kathy or I could stop him. Horace was out more than he was in and reeked of cigarettes. And there were several fistfights between Derek and Lenny, who taunt each other with "busts" about their family's economic standing, issues of hair, whether their mothers work, and who's dirty and who's not.

I'm so tired. ■

As our reading circle grew, so did the intensity of our discussions. During all of our "reading" times there was an incredible amount of talking. We would read a few paragraphs and then talk for many minutes. I would continue to read and either I or one of the boys would interrupt with a comment or observation. I worried that these constant interruptions would so fragment the flow of the text that they would lose the sense of continuity of the story, but it was very difficult to stop them from calling out their comments. I began to realize that this talk was providing many things for us. It was allowing the boys to express themselves, to say what they thought. It was providing a structure that was encouraging them to ask questions that were important to them. Our reading circle talk was also allowing me to get to know the boys, their interests, and their individual approaches to learning. And this talk was bringing us closer together as a group. We were creating a space in which we sat close together and shared ideas.

At the same time, I had deep concerns about the ways in which the boys dealt with differences in race. In mid-October I learned that a new student would be joining us.

Oct. 18

At 2:30 this afternoon I was informed that a new student and his father were on their way to my class. Cruz will be the only Latino student in this class. I'm worried for him. There is so much negative talk about race in this class. Negative talk and stereotypical "cuts" and comments. Racism and its effect on these kids is played out in many ways. Derek and Lenny frequently argue. They talk about each other's "curly hair" and "mothers on welfare," and use racist terms to insult each other. I have heard from both the white and the African American kids stereotypical statements about "Chinese people" and their alleged access to money upon entering the U.S.A. The boys also talk about Puerto Ricans as being "good with knives" and as being difficult to beat in a fight. I've tried to talk about stereotypes, and answer some of these allegations and comments when they come up, but I mostly feel unheard at these times. We have to find a way to have structured talk about race and stereotypes, maybe through our reading, like *Julie of the Wolves* (and then maybe *Roll of Thunder*). One more thing about race in 7–3. These boys are physically polarized from each other in this class. Rasheed, Derek, Reggie, and Robert, who are all African American, usually sit next to each other on one side of the room. Patrick and Dean, the two white students who attend consistently, sit next to one another on the other side of the room. The other students are in and out and sit by themselves when they are in. So, I am concerned for Cruz, but I can't help but think his presence will enrich the class.

Welcome Cruz.

Welcome and good luck. ∎

Derek and the reading of *Sign of the Beaver* helped us to name race. He was able to tease about the term "white boy." He seemed to be testing the parameters of this issue.

Oct. 29

More good days. Little by little our periods of cooperation are getting longer and more frequent. Today, Rasheed and Derek asked if we could read. Our reading times are beginning to be a sort of barometer of the progress we are making as a group. I feel like we're getting to know each other. I'm seeing Derek's sense of humor and Rasheed's love of facts when told to him in a good story. Lenny and Patrick always want to connect past history with current events. Dudley focuses on the scientific. *Sign of the Beaver* is a book about the relationship between a Native American boy and a white boy in the 1700s. They come to depend upon each other, to become friends. It is written from the white boy's perspective, and I have questions about that, but today we used these questions to talk about point of view and stereotypes. We also talked about how the lives of Native Americans changed with the coming of the Europeans. We talked about what it means to be from different cultures, and how that might impact on friendships. I'm still trying to establish the ground rules in this class, to develop a routine. But, reading *Sign of the Beaver* seems to be a period that binds us. ∎

During our sixth week together, we began to read *Julie of the Wolves*. This book is about a thirteen-year-old Inuit girl who has run away from a difficult home situation and who now must depend upon a pack of wolves for her survival on the Alaskan tundra. I had ambivalent feelings about reading this book with my students. My fear was that these boys might not want to read about the adventures of a girl. On the other hand, I thought that the heroine's struggle in the wilderness might capture the boys' imaginations. I also thought that they might be interested in studying Alaska, her people, and the animals and geography of the Arctic. What I did not expect was how the reading of this book provided opportunities for a wide range of discussions. They were very interested in the fact that Miyax, the heroine, was married at thirteen. They were even more interested that she was running away from her husband because he wanted to have sex with her. The boys up to this point had talked a lot about sex, usually with great bravado and slang. They often use this talk about sexuality to tease each other or to appear to have experience. Their talk was full of misconceptions and wrong information, but their banter was so quick and loud, I had trouble being heard. In our reading circle we began to talk about some of these issues.

Nov. 8

The boys were surprised to find out that Miyax was married. She is their age. They began by talking about him (her husband) "doing it to her." They bantered back and forth for several minutes, laughing and trying to outtalk each other. I interrupted them by telling them that there were some adult themes in this book and that I thought they were old enough to read and discuss these issues. I said that they would have to show some maturity, though. I told them that we could talk about sex, but that they can't be silly and they can't tease each other. They can ask questions, but if they don't handle the conversation maturely, we stop talking and we stop reading this book. What followed was a discussion of the age at which humans could conceive, questions about menstruation, what happens to boys during puberty, and the birthing process. They did keep sliding back into teasing and giggling, and I spent a lot of time refocusing them, but taking these subjects straight on seems to be the way to go. These guys actually listened. I think they also learned a little about how to find answers to difficult questions.

Nov. 9

We had a really great reading period today after Art. We were in a circle, eating crackers, trying to ignore Lenny's incredibly rude behavior. He left for a little while, during which time I lectured the boys about how they let themselves become manipulated by someone else's behavior. I had pleaded with them to ignore Lenny's inappropriate behavior if he should return. He did return and they tried their best to ignore him. I yelled at Lenny. I told him that I was disappointed in his behavior. I told him that we were at a really exciting part of the book and we'd like it if he stayed but that we weren't going to be distracted. He actually stayed! He pulled a desk up next to me (pushing Bobby aside), and we read. We read and we talked through Julie's hunger, and her need to nurse from Amaroq, her partaking in the caribou hunt and feast, and her fear of the wolves' leaving. We had wonderful conversation. It was a very close feeling. Lenny was very quiet, listening and watching me as I read. Rasheed shared my book on my other side, even though he had his own. Rasheed continues to follow this story intently, constantly asking for clarification of the action and the relationship of the wolves, which helps us all. Derek has a clear understanding of the vocabulary in the book, both English and Inuit, and uses both regularly. Patrick now reads along, although he still tells me he hates reading (I wish he'd get his glasses). Dean sits quietly, but, I think, listening. Reggie still makes noises and tries to have side conversations. How do I capture Reggie's interest? Bobby IN the circle! Edward there, but not really present.

But still, eight of us were there, and together. Yes, together.

Dec. 5

Oh, we had a funny afternoon today. I was trying to read a handout about Washoe (the chimp that signs). Patrick and Derek had wondered why, if we're descended from apes, don't apes talk, or why we do? Hence this handout.

But it was 1:30, right after lunch, and these guys would not settle down. The usual name calling, discussion about a fight that took place a week ago, who's stupid, etc. My voice was not being heard above theirs. Finally I handed my paper to Derek (they each had a copy) and said "Here, Der, you try. I'm going to take your seat. . . ." He got up immediately and asked, "Am I gonna be you?"

"Yes," I said, "Be me."

"Can I speak Gussak?" he asked, and a twinkle came into his eye. *Gussak,* we've learned from reading *Julie of the Wolves,* is Inuit for *white person.*

"Yes," I said, thrilled by his use of Inuit.

Well, Derek had us rolling on the floor. Every kid was riveted toward Derek as he became me. He adopted my gestures, my tone, and my accent. I have no idea what we learned about Washoe, but we had a hell of a good time. ∎

Sometime during the middle of January I introduced them to the book *Roll of Thunder, Hear My Cry* by Mildred Taylor. This book tested the threads of our very fragile community. As I handed out the books, I explained that it is about an African American family living in Mississippi during the 1930s, struggling to keep their land, while most of the African American families in this town are sharecroppers. The story is told by Cassie, a girl of about nine or ten years. We read the back cover together and talked about what was happening in the United States at that time, focusing on the denial of civil rights for African Americans and the struggle to change unjust conditions.

Lenny stood up and told me that he was not going to read "that stuff." He said, "I know about that stuff with the KKK and how we [African Americans] were treated, and I ain't reading about it 'cause it makes me mad." I made several attempts to explain that I know that period of history is a hard one to talk about because such awful things happened, but that I feel strongly that it's an important part of American history and that learning about how people make change is something that we need to be just as aware of today. But Lenny's voice was much louder than mine, and he was becoming more adamant about not wanting to read this book. "What do you want to make us read this for, Ack? [Ackerman]. You know it's gonna make me really mad. What white people did and all."

At the same time, Derek began to speak up in favor of reading the book. He said, "It's about time we read about what happened to us. So what if it makes you mad, it happened, didn't it?" The debate continued among the African American students. The white students were quiet. I think they felt that they didn't really have a right to enter into this discussion centered around what they perceived were African American issues. I was becoming very nervous about reading the book. What this class did not need was more conflict! But this argument had worth in my mind. Their debate was focusing on historical events. I was finally able to convince Lenny to settle down by asking him to just listen to the beginning of the story, get to know the Logan family a little bit, and then decide if he wanted to read the rest.

We entered into this book cautiously, but immersed ourselves in controversy from the beginning. And from the beginning, much of our talk revolved around the issue of black/white friendships. Jeremy is a character in the book who is white and who wants very much to be a friend to the black Logan children, going against the will of his family as well as against the population of the town. The boys seemed to be as conflicted about this issue as the Logans and Jeremy. One of the African American students, Robert, made comments about how it was OK for Jeremy to be their friend.

Rasheed said, "It was just too much of a risk for Stacey Logan to be his friend, even if he wanted to."

Derek said, "I'm just going to wait and see how Jeremy really turns out."

Lenny several times seemed irritated that we were having this discussion at all, claiming that "Stacey could hang with anyone he wanted to. It ain't up to no one else but him who he wants to hang with."

Patrick, who is white and who had not spoken during the initial talk about reading this book, repeatedly asked questions such as, "What if you think about something one way and your parents think about it another way, kinda like that Jeremy kid?"

To this Shaheed replied, "If what you're thinking is right, it don't matter what your parents think. Not about this stuff, anyway."

Questions about the historical accuracy of the novel arose constantly. We talked about the large landowners and their relationship to the night riders and to the people who made laws, particularly the Jim Crow laws. Derek asked, "How could people hang with those Jim Crow laws?" Patrick wanted to know if "white people could really force blacks to give up their land." Shaheed asked, "How come the people who were share-croppers didn't just leave?"

Every reading and every conversation brought us back to history. Each time someone made a comment, someone else voiced an opinion. Sometimes the debate got heated and their voices became loud, but I was not as fearful of their becoming physical during these arguments as I was during their times of "busting" on each other. In fact, I began to notice that during these discussions, the boys' opinions and contributions to the talk were not clearly defined by race any more. Nor did they necessarily sit next to a person of the same race.

On a cold morning in February, Derek warmed our hearts by making this pronouncement as I was handing out *Roll of Thunder:* "You know, Patrick and Dean are the first best friends I ever had that are white." In March, Patrick and Robert told me that they secretly hung out together outside of school now, but that they weren't sure it was a good idea for other people to know about it.

This class never became a place that was comfortable or easy to be in. But there were some turning points that helped to create our very deep feelings for one another and the common knowledge that our class was a place where we could bring our thoughts, opinions, and feelings about issues that have enormous significance in all of our lives. The first of these was my constant reiteration that I was staying with them no matter what, that I was their teacher until June, and that I was the authority in this room. When, in the second week a few of the students questioned my authority to "tell" them what to do, saying, "You are not our mother, we're not yours," I emphatically told them that, "You are indeed mine. You are mine until June. *Late* June." It also became apparent that my insistence on specific structures was important to their sense of order, even if I frequently was unable to implement these in a way that would include everyone. I insisted that those who were in the reading circle were those who would get our attention, our eye contact, our responses. I struggled and increasingly won the help of those in the reading circle to help me enforce this norm. So, if the boys wanted to feel included, they had to do it our way.

I feel strongly, too, that the significance and quality of our time in the reading circle was heightened by the kinds of literature we read and by how our time reading together was so closely linked with our times of talk. With each of the three novels we read, our talk became more focused, and our community a little tighter. With *Sign of the Beaver* we established that we were going to listen to one another and share ideas. We also established that I wasn't going to censor conversation but that our conversation was going to have some parameters. Reading *Julie of the Wolves* provided us with opportunities to talk about issues concerning sex and sexuality, friendship, trust, and responsibility. The talk that evolved from reading these books often felt risky to me. Our conversations about sex, menstruation, puberty, and racism always made me nervous. I wondered on a daily basis if the boys were going to be able to have debates without fistfights. And I worried about how the administration would view our forays into these often taboo topics. But our reading circle became a space that provided enough safety to talk about issues these boys confronted everyday. The conversations served to alleviate fears and bring us closer together. Our talk served as a means to bridge our differences and to discover our commonalities. And so this risky talk helped—not only to build our community, but also to bring it closer together.

Derek, Patrick, Dean, and Rasheed come back to visit now. They frequently come together, black and white, and they always ask about the books. Every time they come they ask with an air of possessiveness whether or not I'm reading them with this year's class. I still have many unanswered questions, and I am continuing to look at how our community was developed and what role literature and talk played in that development. Hopefully, Rasheed, Patrick, Dean, and Derek will continue to come back and help me with my inquiry into community.

Bibliography

George, Jean C. 1972. *Julie of the Wolves.* New York: HarperCollins Children's Books.

Speare, Elizabeth G. 1983. *Sign of the Beaver.* Boston, MA: Houghton Mifflin.

Taylor, Mildred D. 1976. *Roll of Thunder, Hear My Cry.* New York: Dial Books.

Es Mí Amiga
Full Inclusion in a Second-Grade Classroom

Judy Heyboer

I am always nervous on the first day of school. On this particular day, my voice trembled a little as I gave my students the classroom tour. Already I knew I had lost them; their little second-grade eyes were glazed over. What did they care about classroom rules or integrated thematic instruction? They were waiting for me to shut up so they could go to work with the sharp new points on their brand new pencils.

Fortunately, an interruption saved me. The door opened and a late arrival bounded in, shouting, "*¡Ya vine!* [I'm here!]"

He received an exuberant welcome:

"Roberto!"

"Roberto's in this class!"

"All right!"

"Sit here! Sit here!"

As one of two students with Down's syndrome participating in a full-inclusion program, Roberto was to be in my classroom all day, every day. I had volunteered for the program because of my experience with "special" children—but only when the other students invited him in did I stop to consider what it means to be "included." I felt confident that we could adapt the curriculum to make it accessible to Roberto and his classmate, Yesenia, and I believed passionately that all students have the right to be in a regular classroom. But how would their presence affect the other children? Certainly the students would become more familiar with people with disabilities, but was there any other benefit in it for them? Just how far would the two be included—would there be a place in the social network for them?

Yesenia

Roberto and Yesenia presented very different challenges to the inclusion classroom. While Roberto was outgoing and impulsive, Yesenia was so shy that her first-grade teacher had described her as an "elective mute." It took persistent coaching from myself and the full-time aide just to get her in the door; she avoided eye contact and would bury her face if an adult spoke to her. Most of the day she sat quietly at her desk, not bothering anyone—except for her apparently unbreakable habit of eating crayons. Health issues aside, crayon eating is not an age-appropriate behavior, and the other students did not appreciate watching their art supplies disappear into Yesenia's mouth.

The previous year, the teacher had responded to Yesenia's compulsion by trying to limit her access to crayons, taking them away by force if necessary. Neither the specialist nor I was comfortable with that approach, but more positive behavior modification programs such as rewarding her for *not* eating crayons had little effect. Finally, we decided to address the compulsion in a more appropriate way, by giving her a bag of popcorn to carry with her and nibble on all day. Almost immediately, the crayon eating stopped.

A few days later, I noticed something interesting. Wherever Yesenia sat, a group of children gathered around her. How sweet, I thought; she's making friends. Such attentive and loyal friends, too, always the first to let the aide know when Yesenia's popcorn bag needed replenishing. Best of all, the group included a student named Patricia, who up to that point had made no friends in the class and had refused to participate in any group activities.

Tall, overweight, and physically aggressive, Patricia had experienced problems in first grade that were only exacerbated by later transferring to a new school where she didn't know anyone. For the first six weeks of my class, not a day went by that students didn't complain about Patricia's hitting, pinching, or swearing at them. Now, there she was, sitting quietly in a circle of girls, joining in their conversation, asking Yesenia ever-so-politely for another piece of popcorn.

Popcorn is inexpensive but not free, so eventually I had to make it a rule that Yesenia could not share hers. By then, however, the friendships were established. In addition to becoming Yesenia's surrogate teachers, Patricia and three other girls, all large like herself, went about everywhere together with their arms linked, making up songs about "*las gorditas* [the little fat girls]." They usually included Yesenia. At the end of the year, Patricia wrote the following story:

> *Cuando yo estaba en primero, les pegaba a los niños. Me enojaban mucho. Ya no.* [When I was in first grade, I used to hit the kids. They made me really mad. Not now.]

Roberto

Roberto never made the same kind of academic progress that Yesenia did, but his improvements were no less dramatic. If anything, his progress was even more crucial, because his poor social skills and physical aggressions had much more impact on the other students.

By mid-November, he had settled into a pattern, Because he slept poorly at night, Roberto would come into class drowsy and sit quietly in a corner or fall asleep. As the day wore on and he became more alert, he would become more active and disruptive. The classroom aide left an hour before the students did, so Roberto's peak energy coincided with the time when one less adult was available to work with him. For the sake of the other students, the consultant would take him to an empty classroom and remain there with him.

Unfortunately, that individual attention was rewarding his behavior and encouraging him to use aggression as a means of communicating his desire to leave the room. Nothing could be more damaging to a full-inclusion program than for the included student to hurt other students. How could their parents possibly support the program if their children were in danger? We needed to control his aggression, and the only way to extinguish the disruptive behavior was to stop reinforcing it. In other words, Roberto would have to remain in the classroom even if he acted out.

It is a tenet of behavior modification that the student will test the limits of a new program before conforming to it, and that was certainly the case with Roberto. The first afternoon that we began the change, the consultant explained to Roberto that if he wanted to leave the classroom, he only had to point to an icon of the other room, but that otherwise he would stay. Roberto responded with a series of increasingly physical disruptions. He pushed books off my desk onto the floor. He grabbed pencils away from students and threw supplies across the room. He shouted over and over again one of the few words he could say intelligibly: "Fuck! Fuck!"

After each outburst, the consultant would confine him to a chair. The students and I continued with our art project. When Roberto would quiet down, the consultant would again offer him the choice of pointing to the icon and leaving the room, or remaining and behaving appropriately. Each time, Roberto refused the icon, but when he was allowed to get up from his chair, he would cause another disturbance. Finally, he grabbed a boy by the neck and pushed him to the floor. At that point, the consultant decided to impose the same consequences faced by any student who deliberately harmed another: Roberto was taken to the principal's office and given a one-day suspension.

The next morning, my students asked where Roberto was. I explained that because he had hurt Samuel, he had to stay home for a day. No one was allowed to be at school who hurt other people. After we talked for a while about other students they had known who were suspended for fighting, one girl raised her hand and said, "I felt very sad when Roberto pushed Samuel."

"Me, too," echoed several others.

As I listened to their comments, I was surprised to realize that they weren't angry with Roberto, only confused. They really liked him, and they didn't understand how he could be so mean sometimes. It occurred to me that they could help.

I explained to them that most of what Roberto did was to get attention. "If you don't like what he's doing," I said, "tell him you don't. Then tell him you don't want to play with him until he stops. Turn your back on him so he knows you mean it."

The next day, the children put my advice into practice. From the beginning, they had invited Roberto into their games, but now they were explicit about their expectations. They celebrated his attempts to participate but his acting out was met with silence.

They must have seen the results for themselves, because they followed the negative reinforcement program religiously. Our school serves a high percentage of migrant farmworker families, so we had a new student join the class nearly every other week (a total of fifty children were enrolled at one time or another through the year). The students took upon themselves the responsibility of explaining Roberto to each newcomer, and by their second or third day in the class, nearly everyone was able to ignore any inappropriate behavior. By the end of the year, Roberto's aggressions had diminished from several a day to less than one a month, and he was able to play with other children both in the classroom and at recess.

A mentor teacher videotaped my class one spring afternoon when the children were selecting free-choice activities after finishing their day's work. Captured on tape is a typical scene: Roberto sneaks up behind a boy who is seated on the floor, and he leans his full weight on the boy's back. The student doesn't even look up from the blocks he is stacking. Roberto stands up again, goes to the shelves and chooses his own box of toys. As soon as he returns to the carpet, another boy kneels beside him and asks to play. Within minutes, the two are laughing hysterically over some private joke.

Clearly, peer pressure was an effective force in shaping Roberto's behavior. It worked because he wanted to belong; he cared about the friendship of his peers. No adult had that kind of influence over him, so it is doubtful that any program but full-inclusion would have been as successful in calming his aggression.

What impressed me the most, however, was the experience it gave the other students. Their community is home to two rival gangs, and I have seen children as young as kindergarten declaring their alliance with one or the other. Although they are regularly exposed to the violence of gang life—in fact, that year one of our third-grade students was shot in a retaliation killing—it does not necessarily discourage them from joining. On the contrary, they may see the gang as their only protection. Some of the students no doubt also witnessed domestic violence or were themselves victims of abuse. For these children, striking out in anger would seem perfectly normal.

Teaching children how to resolve conflicts peaceably and how to walk away from an aggressive challenge is not easy. A curriculum can't take the place of real life. Roberto provided my students with an opportunity to practice those skills. They learned first-hand not only how powerful a force peer pressure can be, but also how it can be used to suppress violence as well as to promote it. I can only hope that some of them will remember as they grow older that in my class it was indeed possible and effective to turn the other cheek.

Progress

Overall, Yesenia showed more promise than Roberto in academic abilities. She was able to count and understood how to add and subtract using manipulatives; with her aide guiding her through the steps, she was able to complete a small number of math problems on worksheets. Most exciting, however, was her progress in literacy.

All the students in the class spoke Spanish as their primary language. Many came from nonliterate families from remote rural areas in Mexico where education simply was not available; one nine-year-old boy who entered school that March had never before held a crayon or a pencil. At the beginning of the year, many students had not broken code and couldn't read independently. On the other hand, some of the students whose parents or older siblings had completed elementary school not only were reading fluently in Spanish but also had begun to teach themselves to read in English. The positive literacy experiences Yesenia received at home balanced out her disability and placed her nearly on an equal footing with some of the other students in the class.

Of necessity, my language-arts curriculum had to be student-centered, developmental, and flexible enough to accommodate the variety of levels and to provide the very remedial scaffolding that many of the students required. At the beginning of the year, I focused on pattern stories to help the students make the connection between oral language and print. These Spanish books were chosen for their rich, rhythmic language and for the repetitions of phrases that made them suitable for choral and shared readings. Yesenia never participated, but she always sat in the very front row, her eyes glued to my face and her mouth hanging open in rapt fascination.

After a few months, we expanded into more complex literature and more individual reading time; the pattern stories remained available to the children as books they knew they could read independently. One afternoon as we were putting the books away to get ready for recess, I heard a voice continuing to chant phrases from one of the earliest stories: "*Veo,*

veo. ¿Qué es lo que veo? Corre, corre, ¡qué te alcanza! [I see, I see. What do I see? Run, run, it's going to get you!]" (Kratky 1989). Yesenia, the "elective mute" of the previous year, not only had memorized the story and retained it over several months time, but also was confident enough to let us all hear her read it.

After Christmas break, the students had enough of a foundation for us to begin writer's workshop. I provided as much scaffolding as possible through word banks, cross-age tutors, and minilessons that gave the students structured cloze stories they could complete. An additional incentive was the classroom computer, where students could type their finished pieces.

It did not take long for the children to leave the scaffolding behind and develop their own styles of writing. While Patricia was writing about her anger in first grade and her friend Anita chronicled the true-life adventures of her little sister, another of the "*gorditas*" was exploring horror stories.

At first, Yesenia showed little interest in writing a story, but as her friends continued publishing and sharing their books, she spent much of her free time looking through the books and listening to the others read. In March, about the time we were studying oceans, she began to dictate stories to her aide. Stories about eating. She integrated both the class theme and her own eating compulsion into her first published work:

> *Un caballo del mar y un cangrejo son amigos. El cangrejo come lechuga. El tiburón come uvas.* [A seahorse and a crab are friends. The crab eats lettuce. The shark eats grapes.]

When it came time for her to share the book in the Author's Chair, Yesenia was too shy to read it herself. She chose a friend to read the words while she showed the illustrations. Although there were a few giggles, her classmates listened attentively and the applause when she finished was genuine. At her end-of-year conference, she proudly showed off the book to her parents, and although she was still too shy to read it, she was able to identify the animals in her drawings.

With her subsequent books, Yesenia received less and less assistance from her aide as the other students took over the role of the teacher. The aide still took dictation from Yesenia and I still edited the first draft with her, but her friends volunteered to help her type the words on the computer, match the words to illustrations, bind the final product, and share the published book with her classmates. Yesenia communicated clearly what they might and might not do with her work and in what ways she welcomed their help. She was also very clear with me, ordering me away and hiding the pages from my sight until she was satisfied with them. She never overcame her shyness in front of a large group, but neither did many of the other girls in the class.

Conclusion

I cannot say that Yesenia would not have learned to read had she not been in the full-inclusion program, but I do know that most self-contained classes for the severely handicapped must of necessity focus on behavior and vocational skills. They cannot provide the same kinds of opportunities to write or as much exposure to good children's literature. Yesenia has continued to progress since leaving my class, and she can now read and write with some independence. I am told that the first time she read to her father, he wept.

If full inclusion is more than just a fine liberal experiment in civil rights, if in fact it is a sound educational practice, then we should expect to see a permanent change among those who have participated. After all, the proof of any learning is the student's ability to extend it beyond the classroom. Yesenia and Roberto had become part of the social life of my classroom—so much so that when my husband, himself a teacher of the severely handicapped, visited us at the end of the year, he could not even pick Yesenia out from among the other girls. But how long would that last?

It has been two years since we were together, and I can say that so far, my students' friendships have survived. As we placed the students with their third-grade teachers, the specialist and I were careful to keep Yesenia's circle of friends as intact as possible, but inevitably some of the girls had to be placed in other classes. Still, I see them together at recess—Yesenia, Patricia, and the other *gorditas*—jumping rope and playing tag. Whenever Yesenia has a problem—a child teasing her or a shoe she can't tie—the others are there to help. Yesenia is still too shy to meet my eyes or answer questions that I ask her, but if one of the younger special education students clings to me, Yesenia steps between us and says, "*¡No! Es mí amiga.* [No! She's *my* friend.]"

Roberto was transferred to another school where he only is able to participate in the regular classroom on a limited basis. His parents at first opposed the transfer because they were so pleased with the success of the full-inclusion program, and they only agreed because the new school is closer to their home. At the end of the school year, the specialist visited Roberto's new school to observe another student. She saw him on the playground—all alone except for one boy who, until he also changed schools, had been with Roberto in my class.

Bibliography

Kratky, Lada Josefa. 1989. *Veo, veo ¿Qué es lo que veo?* Carmel, CA: Hampton Brown.

Lee's Story
Living with Loss

Janine Chappell Carr

Separation
Your absence has gone through me
Like thread through a needle.
Everything I do is stitched with its color.
    W. S. Merwin

It was a Monday morning in March. My room was quiet. I was still holding on to the solitude of my weekend as I anticipated the hectic pace of thirty-two first-grade children. 8:00 A.M. Thirty minutes of calm left in the day. Then the door opened and in walked Lee.

With her blonde hair and brown eyes, she was so tiny. First graders are never very big, their shoelaces as long as they are tall, but she was especially petite. It seemed to me that she hadn't grown much since the beginning of the school year when her aunt had spoken briefly with me about Lee's parents. Her aunt's home seemed to be the only stable place for Lee, and her aunt was a single parent with a four-year-old and a baby. As we began our year together, I discovered that Lee had more bumps, bruises, scrapes, and aches than I had ever imagined one child could have.

She was not alone. Recently my principal shared our school's profile information with our staff:

Almost 60 percent of our 1003 student population is Hispanic; 10 percent African American; 27 percent white; and the remaining are mixed Native American, Asian, Pacific Islander, and Filipino. Our students are lovable, affectionate, and have many social and interpersonal needs. One of their greatest needs is family cohesion. As I visit their homes, it is common to see single-parent households, households with numerous unrelated people living jointly, and households lacking basic furniture such as beds, couches, and dining tables. Our school receives the highest percentage of Chapter I money in our school district by virtue of AFDC this year and will be receiving the greatest percentage of Title I money next year according to the new poverty index. 73 percent of our families live within the poverty level based upon the federal government's standards.

The Classroom Community

Community is at the heart of my teaching. Even when I struggle to really know thirty-two children on a year-round, multitrack schedule, I believe children's needs are best met within a community that cares about them. But still I constantly question myself, How can I help the children and families in my classroom to feel like they are part of a community? How do I listen to, talk with, and show my first graders that I care enough to help them through the difficulties they face? What is service to these children amidst some very complex issues? Every day when I walk across the school grounds to my classroom door, I wonder at the intensity and complexity of the lives that come to one small classroom, and I remind myself to be as clear in my thinking, listening, and decision making as I possibly can be in the hours that we are together.

Thus, one of my hopes for Lee and the rest of these children with real life struggles is for them to come to a classroom every day that feels like a home, a place to be loved and a place to love—a place where they can share laughter and tears and write about their lives that are stitched with the threads of absence, loss, and separation—a place to learn, together, as a community.

Lee's Sorrow

On that March morning, Lee was early and wanted to hang her backpack on her chair before she went out to the playground.

"You know what?" she asked.

Oh, I thought to myself, I'm not quite ready for the weekend stories. I'm not even ready for this day yet.

"I saw my daddy this weekend," she continued.

"How was that?" I asked, thinking, perhaps this won't take too long. Lee came close to me, to the table where I was working.

"Good. I asked him to stop drinking and he did."

This wasn't going to be quick. Time to listen closely. I knelt down in front of her so I could see her eyes. Some of her blonde hair had been pulled up into a little ponytail on top of her head, the rest fell in wisps around her face.

"Was this just recently?" I asked her.

"It was before he moved to this house. He used to drink a lot, then he only drank two bottles a day at the house with the upstairs and down-stairs, then one bottle. Now he doesn't drink at all. He still smokes even though I asked him not to do that. At least he doesn't drink any more."

"Was he OK this weekend? Did you stay with him?" I needed reassur-ance as much as she did.

"Yeah, but he had to leave for work before we could go to the beach. He bought me these new shoes though." She turned her foot in circles for me to see. She wore little denim sandals with pink embroidered flowers on the toes.

I looked down at her feet. "Those are fancy," I told her. "They look summery. Pretty soon you'll be able to wear those without socks."

"I feel like I don't have any shoes on. I can't feel them at all!" She smiled. We both admired her shoes. Perhaps everything was fine after all.

Lee continued. "I haven't seen my mom for ages. She finally brought me my Christmas presents yesterday. But I didn't see her. I was at Girl Scouts when she came."

I sighed. Everything was not fine. Christmas presents in March? "What did she bring?" I asked.

"A Polly Pocket that lights up," Lee answered.

"How did that make you feel?"

"Good. But I miss my mom. I've been living with my aunt since I was a little baby. I call her Mom now."

"Your aunt loves you a lot," I reassured her. "I'm glad she cares for you and that you have a safe home with her."

"Yeah. She just tells me to remember the good times."

I could see the tears pooling in her eyes.

"You know why I don't live with my mom and dad?" she asked me in a shaky voice. "'Cause when I was little they couldn't decide where to live anymore and they split up to live in different houses so I went to live with my aunt."

Her melancholy eyes were not pools anymore. Now she shook and cried deeply. I gathered her tiny self in my arms and spoke softly to her. She felt so little.

"I know you hurt inside, honey. I know you miss your mom and dad."

"My dad wants my mom to come see me."

"How long has it been since you've seen your mom?"

"Years and years. She calls on the phone and says she's going to come see me, and then she gets busy with lots of work on the weekends and can't come."

"I'm so sorry, Lee," I said to her, holding her close for a quiet minute. Her trembling seemed to ease a bit. "Maybe you should get out your writing tablet and write about what you feel. Sometimes when I'm very sad and I hurt inside, that's what I do and that helps me. Maybe it will help you too. What do you think?"

Lee nodded. We wiped her tears together.

"Why don't you get your writing tablet and find a cozy place where you can write before the bell rings. I'm going to sit here with my writing notebook and do some quiet writing too."

Writing That Heals

Lee retreated to the library corner and snuggled down into the pillows to write, while I began to capture our conversation in my own notebook. We settled into the quiet of our thoughts. The few minutes we had before 8:30 ticked away.

"I'm done," Lee announced, her voice breaking into the words on my page. She laid her tablet on my notebook for me to read.

> I miss my mom and my dad. And I used to live with them but my mom and my dad didn't know where they were gonna live so I had to go live at my aunt's house.

The bell rang. It was time to start. I sighed. I wondered what other stories would greet me at the door.

Later that morning when we gathered to start our writing time, I read aloud excerpts from my writing notebook, penned during the weekend while I had a few quiet moments away from the rush of Room 12. I share my writing life with my first graders because I want them to understand that on my best days I pay attention as I "go through the world, and the world goes through me" (Graves 1994). I want them to know I have a need to capture in words what I notice or what is happening in my life. It occurred to me while I was sharing my notebook, looking at my latest entry of my conversation with Lee, that perhaps she and I could tell the children about our "before school" talk.

I felt hesitant about asking Lee to do this. I realized these were private hurts and possibly that's how they needed to stay. I, along with her writing tablet, had already been her listener this morning. Perhaps that was enough. I know how much little ones generally want to please their teacher, to say the right thing, so I had to think. I was also concerned for the other children—the would-be listeners if Lee indeed decided to share her troubles. This was emotional stuff for six-year-olds. Was it fair to ask them to experience these troubles without warning? I thought, how do I feel as an adult when I am in a similar situation and something very private is shared unexpectedly?

I debated what to do in that one moment: Trust that we care enough about each other at this point in the year that we are ready to share her sorrows, or tuck them away and find another way to talk with the children about "leading a writerly life" (Calkins 1994). I chose my path and quietly asked Lee what I hoped would allow her to make the decision.

"Lee," I said, "how would you feel about sharing our conversation this morning?"

I waited while she decided. She was willing. Thus, Lee's aches became public that morning:

LEE: My mom and dad don't live together.
ANNA: Mine don't either. I live with my mom, and my dad lives in Hawaii.
MARIE: Are they divorced?
LEE: [*Shakes her head yes.*]
ANNA: My dad calls over at my grandma's sometimes and asks if the children are there. When we are, we talk to him for a few minutes.
LEE: It makes me really sad. But then when I wrote about it, I just forgot it.
JANINE: I suggested to Lee that she write and perhaps that would help.

That's what writers do sometimes when they are sad and trying to figure out their lives.

MARIE: Yeah. They just write it down and it's gone from their head.

LEE: That's what I did and I'm not sad anymore.

I listened intently. Our community felt strong. We felt like a family that cared for each other. I contemplated Anna's immediate empathy for Lee. There was a place inside Anna that knew Lee's struggles, because she had experienced separation herself.

The Cost of Separation

In her book *Necessary Losses,* Judith Viorst (1986) writes eloquently about the effects of separation on a young child—specifically, separation from the mother. "The cost of separation is high," she concludes. Viorst continues,

> Severe separations in early life leave emotional scars on the brain because they assault the essential human connection: The mother-child bond which teaches us how to love. We cannot be whole human beings—indeed, we may find it hard to be human—without the sustenance of this first attachment. (19)

I realize that as resilient as Lee and some of my other first graders seem to be, certain aches may be there for a lifetime. As Viorst notes, "When separation imperils that early attachment, it is difficult to build confidence, to build trust, to acquire the conviction that throughout the course of our life we will—and deserve to—find others to meet our needs" (21).

As the children left our gathering place to go to their own writing that morning, Marie stopped Lee and asked her if she would read her writing to her. By that time, some three hours after our early morning conversation, Lee had forgotten some of it, so I read with her. We talked about her writing. She had written what had happened, but not how she felt about it. Perhaps, I suggested, that could be her entry for her writing time. Apparently that felt right to her because her next piece of writing conveyed the sadness she felt:

> I feel sad because I don't live with my mom and my dad because my mom and my dad broke up so I had to go live at my aunt's.

Lee's needs are many. She hurts easily. Particularly at the beginning of the year when Lee and I were first making our connections, a minor scratch was cause for tears, uncertainty, and attention. She conjured up endless ailments so she could visit Mrs. Hoglen, our school nurse. "This one's going to take some time," I thought to myself. I understood that Lee's aches went deeper than the ones I could see.

Literary Allusions That Comfort

More recently, there was a day in April when I walked out to the playground after lunch to pick up the children from recess. It had been an especially hectic morning, a before-school conference for me, kids not solving problems well, an unexpected visitor to our classroom. When I greeted the children, there was Lee, holding her arms around herself, crying.

"What is it, Lee?" I asked her.

"I miss my two dogs and my cat," she said, with real tears and real hurt.

"What has happened to them?" I didn't completely understand what she was talking about.

"They died," she answered.

I remembered that Lee's pets had died. She had written earlier in her writing tablet about this, also. It was the frequency and degree of hurt she still expressed over her lost pets—whether outside on the playground or through her writing tablet—that troubled me:

> My dog died because a guy on a motorcycle left my gate open and my dog ran out of my yard and got ran over.

"Hold my hand as we walk in," I said to Lee, "and perhaps we can say a few good words about them as we walk to the classroom, just like the little boy did in *The Tenth Good Thing About Barney* [Viorst 1971]. Maybe that will help."

I use "literary allusions" (Atwell 1991) often in my teaching life. I look for openings in our conversations to share wisdom, humor, life's lessons, and questions from the wonderful literature that I have read with them. I want them to understand that even at six, they are not alone in their feelings. I step back and listen carefully for literary borrowings in their conversations, recording them in my notebook, contemplating what stories have woven themselves into the tapestry of their young lives. Who do they turn to when they are trying to make sense of the world around them? I listen to these children and say, "Other children, and adults for that matter, have felt this way too." And while I am doing this, I am often searching through my mind for a book, a book that will listen, hold their hands, and give them hugs long after I am gone.

I still find great comfort in Hans Wilhelm's *I'll Always Love You* (1985) when I long for our family mutt, my childhood pet, Tippy, and share with children how I felt when she died at eighteen years of age. I wasn't home from college yet when my brother-in-law, Rick, buried Tippy in his field, but I felt the same sadness as the little boy in Wilhem's story when he buried Elfie.

I was thankful I could reach for this same book when Lee and Josephine needed comforting because they, too, had lost a pet that was dear to them. When Patty, perched on a chair, read to the class with such sadness about her dog who had been taken away from her to the dog pound, both Lee and Josephine gave a similar gift of empathy to her:

LEE: One of my dogs who died, his name was Spike. When I came back from school he was gone. He got hung 'cause he had a choker collar on, and he went to chase a cat, and he got hung up and died. My dad told me when I got home from school.

JOSEPHINE: We know how you feel, Patty. Remember at the beginning of the year? My dog got hit by a car. A dog is like a friend. He knows how to make you feel better. He's not a human being, but he's still a friend to you. When Miss Janine gave me that book, *I'll Always Love You,* it made me feel better.

I admired how closely they listened to Patty, how intuitive their ability to comfort her, to understand her, as they shared their own losses. There is a solace in knowing that others have similar feelings and experiences in their lives. I want my first graders to know this early on. It may be the words they can hold onto for a lifetime.

Writing the Stuff of Our Lives

Holding on to the words of others, composing our own words with needle and thread as we stitch the colors of our lives, creating a place where we can listen to each other and share the aches—these are the ways I listen to, talk with, and show my first graders I care about them and want to help them through the difficulties they face. When Lee writes, "I miss my mom and my dad," and "My dog died because a guy on a motorcycle left my gate open," I say to her, "This is the stuff of your life. You must write about it."

And write she does. Just last week I took home the "middle of the year" writing pieces my children had done for their school portfolios so I could sit and read them, wiggling my way into their lives through their writing. Daily, I hold their conversations in my hands to examine after I make fast and furious notes in my notebook, but I need a quieter space to reflect on what they are telling me through their writing. I had asked them to write about something important to them—something they loved, or remembered, or felt—something they noticed or that was significant to them. And so as I read that night, I settled into Lee's thoughts. They were all too familiar:

> I don't live with my mom and my dad so now I live with my aunt because my dad and my mom don't have any money. That's why I don't live with my mom and my dad. I miss my mom and my dad.

Her April words were reminiscent of those she wrote in March, which reminded me of her February writing:

> I miss my mom because I don't live with my mom. Love, Lee

which echoed those of January:

> I feel sad 'cause I don't live with my mom and my dad.

"Loss can dwell within us all our life," writes Judith Viorst. For Lee, this does not seem to be one of Viorst's losses that "must be counted among our necessary losses in order to grow," but rather an absence where "the pain is unimaginable. The healing is hard and slow. The damage, although not fatal, may be permanent" (11). I already see the loss in Lee at six. She not only feels deeply the loss of not living with her mom and dad, but also the loss of her pets. Her kindergarten teacher wrote on the back of her first-grade card, "Nice, eager little girl; easily upset." There are those days when I walk out to the playground after lunch recess and see Lee, with tears, needing—needing my hand or a hug as she tells me she misses her two dogs and cat that died—and I simply don't know what to do. I don't always know how to console a loss that goes that deep.

Yet there is still a lot of hope in this little girl. Even though there are tears, there are many, many smiles—for me and for her. In her journal, we spent several weeks corresponding about her wish for it to rain so she could get out there and jump in the mud puddles—inspired by Henry and Mudge's adventures in *Puddle Trouble* (Rylant 1987). Her love affair with Mem Fox's *Shoes from Grandpa* (1989) gave her such confidence as a reader that when she read it to me she said, "I'm really good at this, huh?" and wrote on our reminder clipboard that she wanted me to get her her *own* copy of the book. I am delighted when she comes up to me and announces, "I just solved a problem all by myself, and I didn't need help from anybody." "I'm so proud of you, Lee," I say to her.

The Most Beautiful Place in the World

What are some tangible ways to address the difficult problems that Lee and some of her fellow six-year-olds are living with? I can only trust that one way is a caring classroom community—a place we have created together—where we care about the bumps and bruises, aches and pains in our lives. For this one year, perhaps I offer a classroom that may be "the most beautiful place in the world" for them, like San Pablo is to Juan and his grandmother (Cameron 1988).

> "The most beautiful place in the world," my grandmother said, "is anyplace."
>
> "Anyplace?" I repeated.
>
> "Anyplace you can hold your head up. Anyplace you can be proud of who you are."
>
> "Yes," I said.
>
> But, I thought, where you love somebody a whole lot, and you know that person loves you, that's the most beautiful place in the world.

Already Lee has plenty to write about. Too much that has already happened in her young life is big and significant. What she is experiencing is more than any six year old should have to. Yet, every day she does. "Your absence has gone through me . . . Everything I do is stitched with its color." It is with delicate threads of great hope that I live and teach with these first graders every day . . . first graders like Lee. Friends by her side, pencil in hand, tablet in her lap, she is leading a brave life in the midst of a loss she feels very deeply.

Bibliography

Atwell, Nancie. 1991. *Side by Side: Essays on Teaching to Learn.* Portsmouth, NH: Heinemann.

Calkins, Lucy. 1994. *The Art of Teaching Writing: New Edition.* Portsmouth, NH: Heinemann.

Cameron, Ann. 1988. *The Most Beautiful Place in the World.* New York: Alfred A. Knopf.

Fox, Mem. 1989. *Shoes from Grandpa.* New York: Orchard Books.

Graves, Donald. 1994. *A Fresh Look at Writing.* Portsmouth, NH: Heinemann.

Livingston, Myra Cohn, ed. 1987. *I Like You, If You Like Me: Poems of Friendship.* New York: Macmillan.

Rylant, Cynthia. 1987. *Henry and Mudge: Puddle Trouble.* New York: Bradbury Press.

Viorst, Judith. 1986. *Necessary Losses: The Loves, Illusions, Dependencies and Impossible Expectations That All of Us Have to Give Up in Order to Grow.* New York: Fawcett Gold Medal.

———. 1971. *The Tenth Good Thing About Barney.* New York: Atheneum.

Wilhelm, Hans. 1985. *I'll Always Love You.* New York: Scholastic.

❊ *Akinamiotak* or *What Goes on the Wall*

Deborah Banks

I am remembering Great Whale River and the Inuit children there, like little seeds unplucked by the wind. They are waiting to look at me when the plane lands, scraping the gravel runway and spitting dirt into a deceptive August afternoon. I am the tentative one, a bit frightened "qallunat" or white person, gratefully welcomed because I bring them knowledge from the south. I am the wise one. Wiser even than their own withered, toothless elders whose brittle bones have known a land I cannot begin to fathom. How can I be wise here?

So my year begins unbalanced. I am given honours I have not earned.

I am standing in my native province 1500 kilometers north of Montreal, looking at the shy Inuit faces watching, watching, watching silently. We are a study: white faces and artificial colours of aquamarine and pinks and orange. Our clothes shriek in a Northern land. Their jackets, their skin, and scuffed boots whisper, "earth."

Markassi is there with the rickety blue pickup truck to take me to my house.

"What about my boxes?" I ask.

"I get those later," he replies, a slow drawl, each syllable stretched toward the horizon. Slowly. Everything slowly. I realize only weeks later that my fast, southern, finger-snapping pace is entirely unnoticed, so why even bother? I learn patience. I learn to be peaceful. Markassi drops us one by one into the sand outside our new homes and quietly disappears.

The town is built mostly on sand and rock. The makeshift runway skirts the shores of Hudson Bay. The ocean itself is forbidding—a curling grey mass roiling and boiling and throbbing with mythology. There is always a brisk wind, I will learn later, and on this first day there are no exceptions. I stand there and look down the line of houses—a neat row of boxes dropped upon the sand, and, off in the distance, the rocky outcrop, the lichen twisting around the rocks where grass should be but never would survive, and the thinning, dwarfed trees scattered along a grey horizon. My eyes take in the other teachers unloading themselves from the truck and slipping through the sand like awkward sunbathers to their respective homes for the year.

My first few weeks teach me a tremendous amount about patience and, certainly, humility. It would seem I am to learn these lessons over and over again.

I meet my Grade Seven class a few days later and study their watchful faces—round and shy, dark skinned and open. I am sure they do not know what to make of me, a teacher in the Arctic wearing skirts, drinking tea with them on the classroom floor, and baking them a pumpkin pie so that they will know its taste for the first time.

What I do not count on is losing my life, my free time and my weekends, totally to them. They arrive at my door on Saturday morning, eat everything I leave on the table or in the fruit bowl, and leave late Saturday afternoon. Often they reappear Sunday morning to save me from myself yet again. It takes me several months to learn how to wean them of this habit so that I have a few hours to myself. I don't know how to tell them, and I certainly don't want to offend them or their parents. After all, this community is small, and in the Arctic, the children belong to everyone.

My Saturday companions include half of my class: Sarah, who fills her pockets with fruit when I am not looking; Daniel and his little sister Annassi; Adamie; Moses, the most silent child I have ever met; Anna; Lucy; Noah; and Mina. Sometimes when I get the door shut on all these little huddled figures in the front entry, they stand and wait for permission to enter further. They come in and sit or chatter in Inuktitut, just content to be in my home while I putter about doing household chores.

The first weekend, all the girls use the bathroom at once. Six giggling girls pile into that room together—each too shy to go there alone, and every one of them too shy to flush a toilet. Their homes hold no such luxuries. Instead they use what is known as a "honey bucket"—a pail with a garbage bag on the inside covered with a portable toilet seat. It is these differences that make me squirm in my skin and embarrass me. How dare I be so fortunate as to have a seemingly endless water supply and indoor plumbing? I know it separates me from them, and I don't like it.

Sometimes I give them my white paper, and they paint for me caribou, ptarmigan, and wolves. Sometimes they will draw the goose they shot or, once, a great grandfather who ran as fast as nine wolves and held his eyes open with little wooden sticks. They tell me about the island that keeps moving away from Great Whale, drifting on the ocean like a lazy piece of wood. Anna tells me about the mermaids in the ocean, and I am a hungry little girl eating their stories. I learn about the spirit on the rooftop of one of the houses, whom everyone but me has seen, and how he keeps dropping rocks onto the tin so no one can get any sleep in the house. Anna has seen him sitting there in broad daylight, right there on the slope, knees bent, a shadow perched on the tiles. They give me their mythology on sheets of paper, and I decorate my walls with it.

I have not been in the Arctic three weeks when the land prods me, prods us all, with a reminder of who is in control. I am to learn more stories later of frozen skin, getting lost on the tundra, and wolf attacks, but early September prepares its own lesson.

Daniel's mother and father have gone fishing for the day in one of the tributaries off Great Whale River. His mother loses her footing and the river sweeps her away. Very few of the Inuit ever learn how to swim. They are afraid of the water. It is full of spirits and monsters and dancing islands.

The community shuts down, and the men putter out of the village in sad little boats searching for Daniel's mother. I stand in my classroom on the second floor and stare out the window. High on the bluff overlooking the huge, rushing river, I see a string of solemn women, quietly weaving and pacing the shoreline, huddled together, pathetically watching their men search.

The school is closed for several days. My principal and several of the male teachers join the search. The rest of us wait. We wait forever.

And that's how long it takes before Daniel's mother is found and brought to the waiting women to prepare for the funeral. The children surprise me with their curiosity, peeking into the windows of the long house beside the school. Inside the women are washing and dressing the body. They say to me, "Deborah, she doesn't look the same."

"Deborah, why is she so big now?" Wrinkled noses squint up at me.

Daniel stands apart with his little sister holding his hand.

The funeral sweeps into the village like a hailstorm, and the houses are emptied of their Cree, Inuit, and white people who filter into the small wooden church to cry and to listen. The blank faces of children and women follow the plain wooden box. Their shrill wailing crawls up the back of my neck into my scalp and somehow comes out of my eyes. I am a little frightened by the screaming; it is so foreign.

We walk slowly through the town. The coffin has been placed on the blue pickup, and we trail behind in the sand to the cemetery in the reedy grass along the Hudson Bay shore.

A few days later, there is life again. A summer shower is over. The grieving slides down into the earth, we go back to school, there are no more tears. My eyes widen to see Daniel laugh in class, reclaiming his giggles and his friendships. There are no monuments to pain. They live. They continue with life because, really, there are no other choices. The land of the Great North shakes its billowing blanket, yawns, stretches, and rolls over, asleep again.

So it should be no surprise that the following Saturday my door swings open to greet Daniel and Annassi. Hand in hand, these two little faces present themselves to me ready to paint stories and decorate my walls.

Moving Marshall

Anne G. Landis

Although I have worked in the same room for twenty years and still cover all academic subjects, my self-contained classroom population has changed in many ways. It was originally a K–6 learning disabilities program; I now teach only first and second graders. Their special needs include learning disabilities, mental retardation (IQ as low as 65), ADHD, a variety of medical anomalies, and numerous emotional concerns. Every year, among my dozen students, I am confronted with at least one who defies classification. Seven-year-old Marshall was such a student.

Marshall was an appealing boy, with cropped, curly black hair and smooth, olive skin. His dark brown eyes could be focused intently on a yellow jacket buzzing near an open window or on a hole gouged in the top of his desk, prompting a raft of interesting and detailed questions that interrupted the current discussion topic or mini-lesson. The next minute, without warning, he might giggle, cry, or dart from the room, wild-eyed with fear. His academic progress was limited by his inconsistent attention span, learning disabilities, and emotional needs. IQ testing placed him in the borderline range of intellectual potential.

I suspect most elementary school teachers have experienced a similar challenge at least once in their careers. However, with the trend toward inclusion and with greater numbers of at-risk babies surviving infancy today, it will become increasingly common for students like Marshall to be found in regular education classrooms.

Marshall's limited attention span was especially evident during writing workshop, which is held for a half hour every morning. My usual procedure for writing workshop begins with a few minutes of quiet thinking time with the lights out. Each student selects the writing equipment desired, then settles at his or her desk. During this time, talking is not permitted. After five minutes, my teaching assistant and I move from seat to seat, asking for topic choices, which we record in the students' folders. Near the end of the period, students volunteer to share their stories either with a partner or with the whole class. By late October, most students have internalized the routine and begin working quickly, some drawing for most of the time, others writing first. Gentle nudges are given when needed, and approximated spelling is modeled and encouraged.

But even into the springtime months, Marshall regularly would sit for ten or fifteen minutes without touching a pencil, looking off into space or poking at bits of lint in the corners of his desk. Moving Marshall was like moving a mountain with a teaspoon. Yet with his fertile imagination, vocabulary, and creative humor, it was inconceivable that he had nothing to write and only occasional pictures to share.

When nudged to write, Marshall became obsessed with pencils. Either he couldn't find his special new red one from the school store, or the point I had helped him sharpen seven times was still not suitable. He was a perfectionist who erased over each letter he printed until it looked exactly right. His pencil episodes often unleashed a flood of tears. I felt so frustrated with the bare whiteness of the page that cracking his writer's block became my daily goal.

In reflecting on my observations, I realized that Marshall did seem to understand that other students enjoyed writing and sharing orally with a classroom audience. He sometimes watched his friend Derrick write about his father's motorcycles and liked to talk with him about his illustrations. He had demonstrated both interest and positive verbal response to Derrick's story during a group-share time: "I like the way you drew the cycle." I began to think about Marshall's obsession with pencils. That evening I called a colleague who was experienced in the writing process. Her advice led me back to Donald Graves (1991).

Graves' article, "All Children Can Write," describes a verbal third grader named Billy. He previously had been taught in a skills-based writing program where correct letter formation was practiced in isolation and had no role in communicating his thoughts or ideas. He thought of himself as a poor writer. In his third-grade class, however, the teacher stressed writing as a process that began with her interest in what Billy knew:

> Billy's breakthrough as a writer came when his teacher discovered his interest in and knowledge of gardening. . . . Although Billy wrote more slowly than the other children, he became lost in his subject, forgot about his poor spelling and handwriting, ceased to cover his paper, and wrote a piece filled with solid information about gardening. Once Billy connected writing with knowing—his knowing—it was then possible to work with his visual-motor and spelling problems, but as incidental to communicating information. (116)

Donald Graves' article led me to an important first step. I thought about what Marshall knew. He was worried about printing neat letters. He said a perfect pencil point would help, and he had a definite idea of the kind of pencil he needed. He had told me over and over that the point did not look the way he wanted. I reasoned that if any writing were to occur, I would have to join Marshall in his world, the world of pencils, and find out more of what he knew. I would have to find a way to get him to talk about, then write about, pencils—because that's where his interest was.

I was concerned about the amount of undivided attention and conference time this might require, and I wondered how often I would need to repeat the process of active listening and nurturing to guide Marshall's obsessions from mind to paper. In addition, I sensed that Marshall knew I was frustrated with his aversion to writing and annoyed with his frequent trips to the pencil sharpener. I knew he often became oppositional when approached by adults. This presented a dilemma for me as his teacher. Perhaps, I thought, he would feel more comfortable with peer support than he seemed to be with mine.

Remembering Marshall's enjoyment of Derrick's stories and the trusting friendship they seemed to have in the classroom and on the playground, I reasoned that Derrick could continue to model confident and meaningful writing. At the same time, I thought that Derrick's slow, quiet voice and nonthreatening manner could encourage his anxious friend to talk about pencils and gradually to begin writing about them. The following day, before it was time for writing workshop. I spoke to Derrick in private.

ANNE: Have you noticed what Marshall does during writing workshop?
DERRICK: Yes. He keeps sharpening his pencil all the time. Then it just

breaks again. . . . He never shares because he doesn't get any words down. Yesterday he got so angry he started throwing things.

ANNE: How do you feel when he gets upset?

DERRICK: I want him to stop yelling. I want to be his friend.

ANNE: I know your friendship is special to Marshall. You have fun together at recess. And Marshall likes to hear your motorcycle stories.

DERRICK: Yeah, he's always coming over to my desk.

ANNE: I wish Marshall could enjoy writing the way you do. He knows a lot of letter sounds and always has a lot to say during share-time. I would like to help him write a story about his pencil and the way the point keeps breaking. But sometimes he doesn't like it when a teacher sits with him. If I gave you some questions to ask, do you think you might be able to help him write down the words he says? You could be his writing buddy.

Derrick agreed to try. He was Marshall's closest friend. Although ten years old and more mature, he was drawn to Marshall's knowledge of the creature world of spiders, ants, and bees, as well as to Marshall's quirky enthusiasm and weird sense of humor. Whenever he finished his own writing, he would rush to Marshall's desk to share—if Marshall didn't get to Derrick's desk first.

As writing workshop began, I recorded in my journal:

> White-on-white again—Marshall is the only one not writing. He fiddles with his pencil til the point breaks, then gets up to sharpen it. The sharpener is noisy; Marshall is constantly out of his seat. I have asked him not to get up again, because he is disturbing other students. Now he just sits and stares—he is starting to get upset.

At that point, I quietly walked over to Derrick's desk. He was engrossed in illustrating a motorcycle chapter he had written the day before. Bending over his desk, I whispered, "Derrick, I notice Marshall has not done any writing yet. He keeps getting up to fix his pencil and bothers other students. Now he is starting to get upset because I asked him to sit down. This might be a good time to try our writing buddy plan. If you come over and sit beside Marshall, I will show you how to ask questions and you can help him write about his pencil."

Nodding to my suggestion, Derrick followed me over to Marshall's desk and sat beside him on a chair I provided. I stooped down to Marshall's level and spoke in a soothing voice. For ten minutes on that first day, Derrick observed my private conference with a sobbing Marshall, his body draped over a broken pencil point.

ANNE: Marshall, I can see you're upset about your pencil. It's not the way you want it.

MARSHALL: Kkk keeps breaking . . . yyy you won't shh shh sharpen it . . . I ccc ccc can't write.

I began verbally sounding out and printing his words on the bottom of his blank paper in large letters, then continued my questions.

ANNE: What kind of point do you like best? . . . Tell me about your favorite eraser. . . . Why did you choose this one?

MARSHALL: This is my favorite pencil. It broke. Would you please fix it?

Setting aside the page I had used for dictation, I offered Marshall a clean piece of paper and sharpened his pencil. With Derrick observing as a trusted friend, I encouraged Marshall to print the first letter in *My*. I reminded him that he printed a capital *M* every day when writing his name and could do it well from so much practice. I proceeded to repeat, one at a time and with exaggerated pronunciation, the most important words in his dictated pencil story. Marshall was able to cooperate with both interest and focus, carefully printing,

My FavRt PenSL ERaSR it broc wd yYou PLeas fx it.

Looking up with a sly grin, he tested me: "What does it say? Can *you* read it?"

I read back his sentence, following word by word with my finger. Ignoring his mixture of capital and lower case letters, I offered encouragement: "You know a lot of sounds. And you copied the word *you* from the word card in your desk."

Marshall looked confident and pleased with his effort. I reasoned that Derrick's presence had diffused his usual opposition to my help and also provided an audience he enjoyed. I continued my questions.

ANNE: How does the point look now that you really like it and it writes well?

MARSHALL: I like it because the eraser fits right on the pencil.

Together, we continued slowly to sound out his verbal response while he printed the sounds he heard:

iLiK it beKs the erasr fts Rt onthe PnSL.

While Derrick patiently watched, I gently pressed Marshall to illustrate his pencil story: "Look at the long, thin shape of your new pencil. If you touch it you can feel it's sharp." Demonstrating, I ran my finger across its red surface from end to end. Marshall listened and watched. Then he gripped the pencil firmly, pressed the point against the paper, and drew two parallel lines, forming a triangle at one end for the point. I resumed my questions.

ANNE: What color is your favorite eraser?
MARSHALL: I like this pink one because it fits tight on the end and doesn't fall off.
ANNE: You know a lot about pencils. You could write your name on it so people will know it's yours. I think Derrick would be interested in hearing more about it.

I moved away, while Derrick slid his chair closer. A grin sneaked onto Marshall's face as he carefully printed his name, then completed illustrating and coloring his story with the support of a trusted and interested writing buddy. Back at my desk, I recorded additional observations and planned my next step. I hoped that during tomorrow's writing workshop Marshall would read his pencil story to Derrick and might even tell his friend of other topics he'd like to write about. Perhaps yellow jackets, or ants.

Just before morning recess, I pulled Derrick aside for a report on Marshall's progress. I wanted him to understand the support that his friendship provided. He said that Marshall had put an eraser in the picture and had colored the pencil light red. Then I planted another seed: "Derrick, you've had a good talk with Marshall today. Having a friend nearby helped Marshall to finish his pencil story. Tomorrow you could ask him to read it to you. I'll bet he will have other stories to tell, now that he knows how helpful you are."

The next day I again took Derrick aside, reflecting on his role as a helper and repeating my suggestions: "Derrick, why don't you ask Marshall to read his pencil story to you today? You can tell him the hard words if he gets stuck. Use your finger to help him keep his place the way I do when we read big books together." As soon as Marshall was settled at his desk, I motioned for Derrick to come over. Then I returned to my desk to observe their interaction.

DERRICK: Where's your pencil picture you did yesterday?
MARSHALL: [*Looking inside his folder and pulling it out.*] Here.
DERRICK: Are you done? It looks like you're done. It's all colored.
MARSHALL: Yeah. Do you like the way I made the point on it?
DERRICK: How about reading it?
MARSHALL: OK.

For a while, Marshall looked at the text without reading. When Derrick reached over to put his finger on the word *My*, Marshall's eyes focused on the word. He read "My" but stumbled on the next few words. Derrick glanced at me nervously. I nodded approval and smiled, pointing back toward Marshall's pencil story, then continued my own writing. After a minute or two I heard Derrick starting to sound out the words. Marshall looked at Derrick's face, then down at the paper. He began to repeat the words, relying on Derrick's beginning-sound clues. He seemed to recall the story he had composed the previous day, connecting his meaning with the printed words and the letter sounds he knew. Derrick had become a focusing buddy and a nonthreatening audience.

Next, at Marshall's request, Derrick retrieved his latest motorcycle chapter and read it to him. I moved to other desks, reminding classmates they had a few minutes left if they wanted to share with a partner before recess. I was pleased with Marshall's progress and amazed at Derrick's buddy skills. As Marshall and Derrick put on their jackets and headed for the door, I offered some thoughts on their success: "You guys enjoyed sharing your stories today. You put your heads together and worked hard on reading. It helps to have a buddy."

The next day, during my weekly lunchtime recess duty, I watched Marshall searching for insects. This was his favorite playground activity. He had noticed dozens of newly hatched spiderlings near small holes in the side of a fence post. "They're in there," he shrieked. I hurried over to share his excitement, amazed by the stream of questions that followed: "Where are their nests? What happened to the eggs? Which one is the mother? What are they going to eat?

Then, in an equally amazing fashion, he began to answer himself with the observations of a scientist, drawing on his prior knowledge: "I think the mother hid their nest in there so enemies wouldn't get them. Look, they're all the same size. The mother must have left. Maybe they eat the eggs after they hatch. They're gonna catch some food in their webs."

Marshall spent the rest of recess tracking the tiny spiders as they skittled around and suspended themselves on their silken threads. Derrick followed him around, peeking inside other posts to see if they could find any more nests. But Marshall did most of the talking and kept up a continuous chatter until the bell rang.

The following morning, I showed the class my shell collection and let them examine a few. We shared the story *Houses from the Sea* by Alice Goudey. I made sure Marshall had two new and very sharp pencils and his favorite eraser before beginning writing workshop. I told Derrick he could work on his own writing for a while to give his buddy a chance to get started. If his help was needed, I would let him know.

Marshall was quickly engaged in drawing. I watched from a distance, then moved to other students' desks for brief conferences. After fifteen minutes, he had filled the page with intricate sketches of crabs and bees and was working on a larger animal and a man with a weapon. His composing was accompanied by various sound effects.

I whispered to Derrick that his friend was ready for a buddy and accompanied him to Marshall's desk. Obviously proud of his work and needing no prompts, Marshall began to describe in detail what was going on, pointing to each character as he told us the story. Through active listening and response, I nudged the storyteller to become the storywriter, at the same time providing a model for his writing buddy, Derrick.

MARSHALL: This is the crab. He's trying to get away. The man is gonna shoot him. [*More sound effects.*] This is the bee. He's going after the anteater and the man's trying to go after him. The anteater is eating ants. Then the bee stings the anteater, bzzzzzzz.

ANNE: You spent a lot of time drawing your characters. I see that the bee has a sharp stinger. I think other people might want to read this. Printing the words of your story would let them know what happens. Let's work on the words together. Which part would you like to write first?

MARSHALL: [*Pointing to the characters.*] The bee went over to the anteater. And then he stung him.

ANNE: OK. Let's write that. *The.* . . . You remember that word by memory. What kind of *T* begins a sentence? Get out your alphabet card and we'll look it up.

MARSHALL: The big one. [*He pointed to the capital* T, *then slowly printed* The.]

ANNE: Beeeee. [*Marshall printed* Be *then looked at me for the next sounds.*] W-en-t. [*I stretched out the words, sliding my index finger from left to right across the line below. He printed* w n t.]

Marshall was able to remember how to spell *to, the,* and *and.* The other words were printed using the phonetic method provided for the word *went.* I had to remind him to use his finger to space between words so it would be easier to read. He completed printing the story:

The Be wnT To The anTeTR and sTyng him.

I ignored the inappropriate use of capital *T,* but praised him for his effort: "You printed your story carefully. You wrote the sounds as you heard them and remembered some of the words by memory. Now other people can enjoy reading your story. Would you like to share it with the class?" Marshall nodded his agreement. I suggested, "Why don't you practice reading to Derrick while we gather everyone on the rug?"

Together, Marshall and Derrick leaned over the page. Marshall was able to reread his one-sentence text while Derrick kept the place with his finger and helped with the words *went* and *stung.* Satisfied with the practice reading, Derrick joined us on the rug. Marshall, taking the Author's Chair, proudly read his bee story to the class as I pointed to each word. Classmates responded positively. Sherry said she liked the drawings best, while Steven told Marshall he liked the story. I asked Marshall what he was going to write about next. He shrugged his shoulders and smiled.

On Monday morning, after a flurry of weekend television retells and yawns from early risers, the class reentered their writing community. Marshall helped himself to a fresh piece of paper. He drew a martial arts scene at the top, adding an attack-deer with antlers, hoofs, and mane. He drew a detailed shark and crab at the bottom, accompanied by the usual sound effects. While totally engrossed in storymaking, he was not yet storywriting.

Derrick had decided to organize a few of his motorcycle chapters into a book and was busy rereading and numbering pages. I helped him listen for voice stops and new ideas to mark the ends of sentences and paragraphs for publishing. When we had finished, I reflected on the help he had given Marshall the previous week and planned the next step.

ANNE: Remember last week when Marshall was upset—we helped him to write and draw his pencil story. You were also a buddy reader when he had trouble practicing his bee story to share with the class. I think he likes having his best friend as a reading-writing buddy. . . . You know how I use my finger to keep the place and say the letter-sounds as we write class stories and read together in our Big Books. You could do the same thing for Marshall. First you could ask him to tell about his pictures. Then you could help him write down the words he says. After he has the story done in words he could read it back to you. What do you think?

DERRICK: OK. First he tells me about the pictures. Then I help him write it down.

ANNE: [*Motioning for him to approach Marshall's desk.*] That's right. When he's finished writing, you can help him read it back.

DERRICK: [*Pulling a chair next to Marshall.*] Hi. What's this about?

MARSHALL: [*Pointing to a figure with crisscrossed eyes and stars around his head.*] He gets hit in the head with the bat. See here's the bat. But he hit this guy with the numchuck.

Derrick looked over at me, unsure of the next step. I wanted to be careful to nudge the buddy-writing process but also to keep some distance so they would not remain dependent on my support. I noted the bat with my finger, then pointed to a nearby empty space. "Hhhh . . . he. What letter do you hear? You can write the big letter to start your story."

Marshall followed my finger, looked up at me with his huge brown eyes, then picked up his pencil and printed *He.* I repeated Marshall's sentence out loud: "He gets hit in the head with the bat." I told the boys I could see they knew what to do next, then returned to my desk feeling hopeful. Derrick leaned over and pointed to the bat. I could hear him say, "Hhh . . . eee gggets . . ."

Marshall continued to print while I circulated to other desks. Just before recess, I returned to see a two-sentence story and encouraged him to read it back to Derrick using a finger to keep his place. I could tell that Derrick had helped with hard sounds such as the *ch.* Although the buddy writer still needed teacher support, the process was working and both boys seemed a bit more confident. Marshall reread his text with his friend's help:

He gts ht inthe Hd wth the Bt He hit wit numchu.

With additional buddy-writing sessions over the next few weeks, Derrick gained confidence in his role as peer coach, while Marshall became a greater risk-taker in recording and reading his stories in print. By the end of the school year, he was willing and able to write labels, signs, simple sentences, and even speech bubbles for dialogue. He taught me a lot about pencils and insects, about trusting and feeling safe. Connecting writing with knowing helped him to see a purpose for drawing his pencil and insect ideas. His desire to share the stories led him to write the words.

Although Marshall's cooperation and confidence had improved during our writing workshop, the frequency of his emotional outbursts and oppositional-defiant behaviors continued on a daily basis with increased intensity. As a result, he was transferred during the next year to an emotional support class in another building. I knew his class would be using a cooperative learning model as well as a process approach to reading and writing. There would be ample opportunities for future practice and growth as a writer, for sharing his stories in a safe and nurturing environment. In my report to the receiving teacher, I suggested that Marshall's frustration as an emergent writer, along with the positive peer support he had received from Derrick, could lead him toward service as a peer tutor for younger students. The confidence and pride to be gained from a leadership role could be just the right fuel to keep Marshall moving.

Bibliography

Goudey, Alice E. 1959. *Houses from the Sea.* New York: Charles Scribner's Sons.

Graves, Donald H. 1991. "All Children Can Write." In *With Promise,* ed. Susan Stires. Portsmouth, NH: Heinemann.

✳ *Reciting "miss rosie"*

Patricia M. Gulitti

The big hand of the clock made its jump past the number one, setting off the bell that clamored throughout the halls and in room 239. It was 2:05. Her eighth-period ninth graders gathered their belongings—books, pens, notes—into their bags. They filed past her desk, discarding their daily grade sheets on top of the class folder. They walked past her like a blur, blending into the green paint of the walls, evaporating through the wooden door. They were free to go. All except one.

"Don't *you* go anywhere," her voice warned.

Johnny's spindly legs slid out from beneath the desk. His piercing green eyes peered up at her. He whispered, "Can I go now?"

"You know the deal we made. You stay until your homework is done," her voice answered. Even. Steady.

His fingers twitched and began a low drumming against the sticky surface of the formica desk. "What's the homework?" he asked.

"You have eyes. Look at the board."

"C'mon. Can't I just do it at home?" He was on his feet now, approaching her as she sat on the cushioned seat behind her stack of books and blue Kleenex. His legs were long and thin. He was much taller than the others; much too tall to still be in the ninth grade.

Johnny's feet hopped back and forth as if he were stepping on hot coals. The pen in his hand was in constant movement; his momentary substitute for a cigarette. He would raise it to his mouth, inhale, and let it slowly descend toward her as if the desk were an ashtray.

"Johnny, you know what you have to do."

"Can't I just do it at home?"

Her brown steady eyes answered, "No."

"*Why?*" he demanded.

"You and I both know that you never do anything at home."

The pen dropped out of his hand—splat—onto her desk. Her eyes studied the edges of its cap, focusing on the tiny teeth marks that marred its shiny plastic.

"I think that you have worked much too hard to blow it now. I am not letting you leave this classroom until you finish your homework." It had been said. It was final.

Johnny sauntered back to his desk, plopped down into the chair, let his feet rest on the book rack attached to the desk in front of his. His fingers fumbled through the heavy green textbook, pushing through white pages of black print.

"What's the name of that poem again?"

" 'miss rosie'."

Silence filled the classroom. Mike came in to copy down the homework from the board. Debbie came in to say her daily "hello." Tim popped his head in the door to remind her to write the announcement for their next newspaper meeting. Johnny stayed silent at his desk.

She stood up. The sound of her boots echoed against the floor as she walked toward Johnny. She sat backwards in the seat in front of Johnny so that she could face him. She could see that Johnny had found Lucille Clifton's poem, "miss rosie."

"Are you going to read it for me?" she gently prodded.

His upper lip quivered. "Why do I have to read it?"

"Poems are meant to be read," she explained.

Johnny took a deep breath. His eyes focused on the page. He then exhaled a string of words, full force, without space for another breath. In her ears they slurred into a sea of monotonous drones. He looked at her, not expecting praise but hoping for release. "Can I go now?"

Her eyebrows raised. "How do I know whether or not you like miss rosie?" she asked.

"What?"

"miss rosie. Do you like her? Hate her? Not care? What's the feeling?"

"*Feeling?* I don't know what I feel about *her*."

"That's the problem—no feeling. That's exactly how you read it. I want there to be feeling."

His left hand slammed the page. "Why do you always have to do this to *me?*"

She began to answer, "Because it's good for you," but swallowed the words before she could say them. It wasn't a fair answer

"Johnny, you can do this. Let me read the poem to you. Close your eyes and try to imagine the woman the poet describes." She moved the textbook toward her so that she could read it right side up.

He closed his eyes. The soft tones of her voice began to paint the picture of the sweet "Georgia Rose." When miss rosie was reduced to a wet brown bag, her voice gained strength as if urging them both to stand through her destruction.

"What do you *see,* Johnny?"

He flashed his eyes at her again. "I see an old lady sitting on the corner with a brown bag of brandy in her hands," he began.

"And what do you *hear*?"

"This old fool mumbling to herself." His fingers picked up the pen again. It tapped, tapped on the page.

"How do you *feel* about this woman, Johnny?"

"*Feel?* She's an idiot! Can I go *now?*"

She pushed him on. "Then read it that way."

"Read it what way?"

"Show me in your voice that you think she's an idiot."

"Really?"

"Yes, really. Don't you want to go?"

Johnny released the pen from his hands. His fingers took hold of each side of the page as if to support his young voice. "When I watch you . . . ," his voice began, rough, scratchy.

". . . You used to be the . . . ," his voice began to waver in the second stanza as if he were running out of steam. Her hand nudged his elbow as if to say, "keep going."

"When I watch you. . . ." He had now reached the moment in the poem that showed miss rosie's destruction. Johnny's hands began to tap in time with his voice, keeping a steady rhythm. Gaining strength.

His eyes began to dance as his tongue rolled off Lucille Clifton's metaphor. His teeth spat out each word like a watermelon pit lodged in his throat: "You—wet—brown—bag—Woman!"

In the space between them she could feel the energy that ran through his veins. Anger roared through the classroom:

"Through *your* destruction . . . *I* stand up. . . ."

His hands broke free from the text, spread themselves out before her. "*I* stand up!"

The moment was his.

She let it hang there in the air just a bit longer so that they could both swallow it. Then Johnny lifted his head from the page. His green eyes glistened as he met hers at the same level. He smiled.

"Johnny, you can go now."

Getting My Bearings
—Well, Maybe Ball Bearings!

Mary Mercer Krogness

One eighth-grade girl waltzed into my language arts class one day wearing a tight-fitting T-shirt with large, grotesque, plastic hands, strategically placed. Emblazoned across her well-developed chest were the words: "I HAVE A HOLD OF MYSELF." The boys' eyes were out on stems; my temples, pounding. As I asked the girl to leave the room, I thought, what a way to begin class!

I was what many would refer to as a seasoned teacher. I had nearly twenty-five years of classroom experience under my belt, had taught urban and suburban students K–8, and had worked with gifted and talented sixth graders. Most recently I chose to teach a language arts/reading course designed especially for those seventh and eighth graders in our middle school who scored at or below the third stanine in reading comprehension and vocabulary on the Stanford Achievement Test and who also experienced a wide array of language learning difficulties. These students were experiencing a multiplicity of personal challenges. I wanted a different kind of challenge, myself.

But this particular episode was one I'd never before encountered. The girl resisted leaving class—muttering and fuming on her way out the door almost as vigorously as she resisted settling down to language learning each day. What was going on with this fourteen-year-old who alternately sucked her thumb in class and yelled out derogatory comments at me? Why did she often become embroiled in spats with any number of students sitting near her? Why was she using her considerable energy to deflect all of our attention away from learning to focus on her bad behavior? I constantly asked myself, "Why can't you get a handle on these recalcitrant teenagers in your language arts class?"

She was not the only one. What *was* going on with these kids whom I so passionately wanted to engage actively in talking, listening, reading, writing, and viewing? Whom I so earnestly wanted to help take charge of the language and their lives? Why *did* they resist learning by acting out in outlandish ways that derailed our class, or by remaining so passive that I asked one eighth-grade boy, "David, do you have a blood pressure? Are you dead or alive?"

Many of the under- and low-achieving seventh and eighth graders are overage girls and boys who had been retained at least once during their school careers. I aimed to capture their imaginations, spark their curiosity, and hook them on language learning: a tall order. Crucial to my hooking them on talking, writing, and reading was getting to know them and their families. Knowing them personally—beyond their academic work—helped me figure out what made them tick. As time passed and trust developed, I often became privy to devastatingly sad times my teenage students had already faced or were facing, often alone and without the benefit of adult comfort and guidance.

I had always telephoned my students' families at the beginning of each school year to build a firm partnership. But never had I realized the importance of constant and positive communication until I worked with what I call resistant learners. When I telephoned my students' families, caretakers, or guardians—which I began doing during the early days of school and continued to do throughout the school year—we talked about our being partners in their children's learning. My students' families and I talked about helping the young people begin to view themselves as successful school learners. Later I chatted more personally with mothers or grandmothers about a student's progress in writing, new interest in historical fiction, concern about a sick grandmother, or fear of failing eighth grade. Through these frequent telephone conversations, we built understanding and trust. My telephone log served as a running record of my communication with my students' families or caretakers.

Telephone Log Samples

Simone, 8/25. Introduced myself to S.'s mother, who at first sounded worried that I'd called so early in the school year. Relaxed and talked freely about her concerns after she found out I was calling to introduce myself and tell her of my desire to work with her and her daughter. Agreed to call me at school when she noticed S. sliding (an old habit). I promised to do same. Will look forward to more talks.

Fontay, 11/3. Talked with F.'s grandmother the second time this year—this time about his improved attitude and noticeable progress in becoming actively engaged during literature discussions or writing conferences. Emphasized his need to be on time to class *every* day! He slides into class maybe two minutes late almost every day. Directly told his gram that Fontay does need to get to bed *by* 10:00 *every* school night so he can work effectively; so he doesn't get wired and act out so much. Grandmother indicated she has struggled with him since Fontay's mom moved out unexpectedly. I suggested seeking help for herself and grandson (only the two of them) by calling one of several mental health agencies in town—all with sliding fee scales. Gave her the names and telephone numbers of agencies. I suspect boy is very depressed with mom's sudden and unexplained departure. How could he not be devastated? Grandmother sounds overwhelmed. She appreciated my call. We'll keep in touch.

Rasheen, 1/14. Just arrived! Came to us from a Cleveland school. To date, Rasheen's been in *nine* schools—two this year! No wonder his academics and self-esteem are suffering. This boy, who's been shifted from one family member to another, is in a state of confusion and anger. He riles classmates and me, thereby deflecting attention away from his lack of skill in reading and writing. I told his aunt with whom he's now living that I was seeking one-on-one reading/writing intervention for her nephew along with the extra, individual help I'm giving him. I suggested he talk with our art therapist to unload feelings that are stopping him from adjusting to his new surroundings and preventing him from learning. She agreed to come to school for a conference next week. I just hope he doesn't move again!

My students' grave emotional burdens regularly precluded their interest in school, their will to learn and excel, and their membership into what Frank Smith calls "the literacy club." Each day I searched to find the right balance between setting a free, easygoing tempo in my five classes and providing a comfortable structure that offered my students and me a framework for learning. But a volcanic sneeze, a late entry into class, a provocative comment, a fight, could disturb—destroy—the delicate balance. Rolling with the punches, yet knowing how and when to rein in the young people before me, inevitably caused me to wonder, worry, and continue searching for answers that often weren't forthcoming.

Many questions about language learning surfaced and gave me pause. What I call a person's language landscape—his or her individual language backdrop—begins to develop when the child hears the language, listens to stories, talks with his or her family, and plays creatively during the critical early, preschool years, the crucial period of language acquisition when a child's mind and imagination are malleable and ripe for making and using language to learn and create. In most cases, my students' language landscapes were sparse. The majority of my kids had not been read to at a parent's knee when they were preschoolers. Many of them didn't remember being talked with, sung to, or played with during that most important time of a child's life.

Graham, an especially alert and bright eighth grader remarked, "We play Trivial Pursuit in American history class. Even my mom don't know the answers to all them questions." He explained further that she didn't know important periods in history or historic dates, titles of famous literary works, or their characters. I couldn't help Graham and many of his classmates recover what had never happened: early language learning experiences that give children a sense of story, sentence, and character; help them build vocabulary; stir their senses; and awaken their curiosity. That time had passed.

Another classroom story speaks volumes. A student was writing about the problems of rote learning in his response to James Clavell's *The Children's Story.* He called me over to read his response. Instead of writing about rote learning, he mistakenly wrote about the liabilities of "remote learning." A symbolic error, indeed. He and too many of his classmates *had* experienced "remote learning" in school and during the many years of reading remediation. Each time they completed a steady supply of fill-in-the-blank or circle-the-right-answer worksheets or trudged through a never-ending supply of what I call connect-the-dots-exercises—isolated skills and drills—they were engaged (or not engaged) in "remote learning." These exercises did not inspire them to wonder or ask questions. And learning to love the language by working their way through Barnell Loft's or SRA's color-coded reading programs was out of the question.

Many of my students, who'd become accustomed to being filled up like so many empty receptacles by their teachers, and who had learned to feel secure while they completed didactic skills sheets and programmed learning kits, became dependent on the stern structure and security of these benumbing exercises. School, for many of these kids, had been routinized, empty. Yet they'd learned to rely on its predictability—its safety. If they were quiet and well behaved, they could hide behind a prescription of skill-builders or dutifully write a line or two about a character in a homogenized story found in one of the reading kits they plodded through. They could usually avoid embarrassment and censure from their classmates and teachers if they just went through the motions of learning. But of course students pay a high price for such a meaningless and uninspired regimen.

Old habits die slowly—my own and my students'. I'd grown accustomed to students getting fired up about learning. During most of my teaching career, I could swing into action without any anxiety and be assured of bringing a class along. In most cases, my students would be buoyed by my enthusiasm and energy for writing or reading or whatever, and they'd become engaged. But this new challenge proved to be very different. Although many of my seventh and eighth graders enjoyed getting out of their chairs to do improvised drama—and some of them eventually were willing and emotionally capable of settling down to read, write, and perform poetry, to make films, to write their own plays, to sit around our writing-conference table and read their evolving scripts, to get into small groups and respond to literature, and to take oral histories from their relatives—they often didn't connect these varied language learning experiences with school work, specifically with English/language arts class. Very likely they hadn't learned to value this kind of school fare because they hadn't experienced it. I remember the day a boy yelled out, "We don't do nothin' in here." When I asked him what he meant, he said, "All we do in here is talk, do drama, read, and write!"

I won't forget the day Meeshi, a seventh-grade student, said, "Mrs. K., my mom wants to know when we're going to do book reports and have tests every Friday." Although Meeshi explained that she liked our class, she expressed her and her mother's anxiety: We weren't doing bona fide school work. I tried not to sound defensive when I explained to Meeshi and her classmates my philosophy of engaging kids in making and using language, not merely filling them up with language skills, assigning book reports, and testing them every Friday. But I realized that what I was saying to Meeshi (intended also for her mother) was not making the sort of impression I'd hoped, mainly because they both had learned to value these sacred cows of the classroom.

Finally, I said, "Meeshi, you're going to have to have faith in me and my teaching. By year's end—maybe before—you can judge what and how much you're learning in here about talking, reading, writing, and thinking—English and the language arts."

Having to help these young people learn to value a rich, but definitely different, language learning experience from what they'd come to expect took me quite by surprise, but it forced me to take stock of my own pedagogy and practice. I learned to spend time gently easing into a project by explaining to my kids *what* we were doing and *why* rather than by assuming they could figure it out. Making transitions between one activity and another was exceedingly difficult for many of my kids, leading me to understand the importance of creating a simple but solid scaffolding for their thinking and making sure to build bridges or transitions between activities. This ensured their understanding and commitment to our work.

I can still hear Latisha shout accusingly: "Ms. Krogness, you skip around too much and don't stick to the subject." Not until well into the school year did I really understand Latisha's needs. She was telling me to help her make connections between, for example, a story character's motives and his or her behavior or actions. In plain English, Latisha was telling me to slow down. She (and many of her classmates) weren't able to shift gears so quickly and make sudden, often creative, and abstract leaps from one idea to another. Latisha was telling me that she was overwhelmed and exasperated by my free-wheeling style.

By paying attention to my kids, I eventually learned to talk more slowly and shift from one idea to another more gradually. I learned to avoid skating off in too many directions, asking too many questions, and assuming that, like students who have read widely, they were able to make certain connections on their own. My students hadn't *practiced* engaging in abstract and creative thinking, initiating questions, offering opinions, or trying on their ideas for the purpose of having intense classroom conversations and debates. For a host of complex cultural, societal, economic, and educational reasons, my kids had not had the same school opportunities that mainstream students, their peers, had had.

Another very important reason my students required a secure or tight framework for learning was because many of them had not developed personal control. Latisha was always teaching me. "Just holler at us—we're used to it," she yelled one day. Latisha was insisting that I rein her in. And she spoke for many of her classmates who often lost control during class.

Instead of merely coping with their emotional baggage, predictably raging hormones, and provocative tendencies, I learned to capitalize on the latter. For example, I'd intentionally play the provocateur. "How many of you love poetry?" I'd ask, knowing that many of them had already had bad brushes with the usual truth and beauty poems they'd heard in school. "How many of you hate the stuff?" I'd ask quickly. Hands would shoot up. Then, before they had time to grouse, I'd hand them Lucille Clifton's poem "Homage to My Hips" and start reciting it with animation and inflection: "These hips are big hips. . . ." Almost without exception this mighty poem would wow them. The girls usually looked smug, like they understood the power of women's hips; the boys were taken aback and looked sheepish.

Poetry finally brought Latisha and me together. Nothing pleased her more than to be excused from our class to browse the library's 800 section, searching for poems that touched her imagination and her heart. Poetry seemed to be the balm that soothed her soul. Not only was I thankful that Latisha was in the library, productively engaged in language learning; I also simply was happy to have a break from her almost daily diatribes. For her final project in language arts, Latisha created a beautiful collection of poetry, her own and those by Langston Hughes, Rita Dove, Nikki Giovanni, Eloise Greenfield, Lucille Clifton, Maya Angelou, and others.

A long time ago I learned that open communication must be central to a language-rich classroom. My students liked what I called my sermonettes. Usually after report cards had been issued, I took the opportunity to talk with them about building intellectual stamina, the staying power that is necessary when learning becomes difficult or challenging—even daunting. And before this conversation had gotten very far, my kids, many of whom had gotten poor report cards that included poor letter grades, poor citizenship grades, and poor effort grades, were promising themselves and me that they would get "all A's the next time," causing me to give another sermonette about reality!

"Let's take one, maybe two steps at a time," I'd say. "If you have a D in science, let's work on raising it to a C. I'll help you do what is necessary to earn that C. Attend the after-school conference in this room, and we'll work together." While I was breaking through the tremendous denial that school failure breeds (I'm gonna get all A's the next time), I was trying to make school success possible and show my students how to gain access to the system. Classroom conversations of this kind were just as essential to my students' progress and growth as talking about their writing or the literature we were reading. Each day that we practiced ways of taking control of language learning by being initiators and generators of ideas, we also practiced feeling better about ourselves in our classroom laboratory, a safe and accepting environment.

In rereading my weekly journal, I can truthfully say that never had I been on such unsteady ground. My journal reveals my constant struggle to find better ways of helping my resistant students take charge; the entries convey my frustrations as well as my fleeting successes and the pleasure I derived, especially when we were working together. Faithfully keeping that journal and having countless conversations with colleagues and friends helped me to reflect, debate, and crystallize what I was doing right and which practices needed to be revised or dropped. Never had I needed to examine myself, my pedagogy, my philosophy, my style of teaching, and my students' different and changing styles of learning so carefully. Never in all my quarter century of being a classroom teacher had I become so convinced of the efficacy of early language experiences, the power of good mental health as it applies directly to a student's school success and general well-being, and the infinitely interesting challenge of being a classroom teacher who learned to be content with planting seeds—the seeds of hope, energy, stamina, and imagination.

Bibliography

Clavell, James. 1981. *The Children's Story.* New York: Dell Publishing Co., Inc.
Clifton, Lucille. 1969. *Good Time Poems.* New York: Random House.
Smith, Frank. 1988. *Joining the Literacy Club.* Portsmouth, NH: Heinemann.

All I Ever Wanted Was to Be a Poet

Maxene Kupperman-Guiñals

Evelyn is crying in my arms, and
Jose has threatened to kill Carmen
if she aborts that "damn" baby, and
Latoya cannot spell the name of her street,
(but she wants to drop out of school), and
Gerald is gettin' high in the boys' room, and
Bobby's beeper just went off so no drug sales
will slip through his greedy, sticky fingers, and
    the principal wants, and
      the dean demands, and
        the guidance counselor needs . . .

All I ever wanted was to be
        a poet.
"Sensitive," they would say, and
"She can certainly turn a phrase like a key in the door."

I would wear poet's clothes
   (velvet jeans and antique kimonos)
   donned with precise abandon
   of tradition and style.
I would slather black mascara on my long, thick
   poet's eyelashes, and
Oily Gauloises smoke would curl from my petulant
   poet's mouth.

Although I'd be, of course,
   a Very Famous Poet,
I'd only give limited readings
     for passionate causes
   in abandoned garrets
   and slightly damp sub-basements

in Paris,
    San Francisco,
       New York, and
  (for mystery)
Pocatello, Idaho.

I would spend selfish, suffering hours eating
    poet's lunches
  of broiled blowfish with endive salad and kir.
No one would cry to me;
    they would cry because of me, for me.
I will appear to be seared by the everyday pain of the
stranger;
I will spend my hours in tortured discussion
  of healing others' wounds,
    hearing others' sounds.

In a world far away,
they would ask for my autograph and disappear.

  No Evelyn crying in my arms, and
  No Jose swearing wildly in my face, and
  No Carmen, stuck in the terror,
  No Latoya, amok in ignorance,
    not Gerald,
      not Bobby,
  no principal, dean, no guidance counselor,
      no me.

Things That Don't Have to Do with English
The Hidden Agenda

Nick D'Alessandro

My students don't always use school the way they're supposed to.

One morning, during what is officially designated as a writing period, I see Hector and Delia writing notes back and forth to each other. I watch for a while and then walk to their tables to read the note over Delia's shoulder. Hector is reluctant to let me see it at first, but Delia reassures him, "Don't worry, he won't tell anybody." They are having a conversation, on paper, about the senior prom in June, a gala dress-up affair that will be held in the garden of a neighborhood settlement house.

They are discussing which lucky girl Hector, the current eighth-grade Romeo, will invite as his date. I pull up a chair and ask why they chose to write to each other. Hector responds, "We didn't want to talk out loud. We did this because we didn't want to get in trouble." Since talking out loud and getting in trouble have never bothered these students before, and since other students are talking out loud, I express mild skepticism and ask if they think this is an appropriate activity for English class. Hector says, "In a way we were working, and in a way we weren't, because it was about things that don't have to do with English." (My long established practice is that personal letters and notes are OK to write in class as

65

long as the student makes a copy in the office and puts it in her writing folder, so the original text can accomplish its purpose. I'm not surprised that Hector doesn't know this. He rarely writes.)

I press further and Delia admits, "We always do this—it's more personal."

Hector adds, "We can have a private conversation without anyone knowing what we're talking about." Both students work (or don't work) in groups of four, and unless they whisper or go into a corner of our small room, they really cannot talk privately.

This goes some way toward explaining why Hector and Delia write to each other, but I think we can look for a deeper and more useful explanation. Anne Haas Dyson (1994) argues that we need to reconstruct what the child writer in school. Children, she says, live in complex "networks of social and political relationships" and have their own reasons for performing certain writing activities that may have nothing to do with official school purposes. She describes a typology of kinds of "social work" that children do in school and that we can observe in their writing and the way they use it.

In Dyson's terms, Hector and Delia are engaging in "social manipulation or regulation," setting "some kinds of peer affiliations against others." They are establishing that they are close friends, that they exchange confidences about other members of their social group, and that their business is so important that it must be conducted immediately, necessitating the note-writing protocol.

Also operating is a classic junior high school social dynamic: in order for there to be an in-group, there must be an out-group. When I ask if anyone else will read their conversation, they agree, "only Tashana," a trusted friend of both students. This, of course, marks Tashana's special status. She is not much interested in boys yet, but she is a sensible, popular student who serves as the confidant of several of the more socially active students.

Whether we recognize it or not, students construct their own social world in the classroom. I have always been uncomfortable with the idea that school is a place for children where the normal rules and concerns of daily life do not apply, which is often a normative assumption of the culture of school. Of course, as an institution serving a large number of people like, say, a prison or a mental hospital, school must be managed according to rules and conventions. But too many schools are places where a student in early adolescence, who is used to making important decisions in his normal life, can go through a whole day without making a single independent decision about what he reads or writes or learns in the classroom. Refusal to do what is expected begins to seem like a real choice. Once, when I was explaining to the class that some parents had complained about our individualized reading program and wanted the whole class reading "classics" together (whatever that meant, as a parent survey we took later revealed), Carlos, an angry, self-conscious reader, complained, "They say they want us to learn to make our own decisions, and then they won't let us make any." A survey the class took home revealed that the books parents thought their child should be reading ranged from Shakespeare and Dickens to Stephen King and Danielle Steele.

Many of my students are used to leading lives of a degree of independence some of us would find astonishing. Our school community is Hell's Kitchen, on the west side of Manhattan, the area between the Hudson River docks and Times Square. The neighborhood, which the real estate agents have begun to call "Clinton," is slowly changing from its tumultuous nineteenth-century past when it was populated by stevedores, criminals, prostitutes, and transient sailors, but the tenements are still settled by new immigrants as well as descendants of the original families. Although our school—a small one containing four seventh- and eighth-grade classes and an ESL group of children from Latin America, South America, the Caribbean, Eastern Europe, the Middle East, India, and China—was planned as a magnet for the whole district, parents in the community began to use it as their local middle school. Our students are almost all defined as "at risk"; we have no entrance requirements, and we accept children who cannot function in other district schools.

Our children come to school already knowing that they are marginalized members of society. They go to movies and watch television voraciously and feed on all the false and true images of life in America. They walk to Times Square and see shining high-rise office buildings and tourist hotels going up daily, and come back to a school that is made up of a few rooms on the top floor of a one-hundred-year-old-building. They know that other schools provide their students with computer rooms, science labs, libraries, and dance studios, while they do without.

Their families, whether birth or alternative, often show a history of stress; poverty, crime and prison, drugs, physical and sexual abuse, neglect, teenage pregnancy, and AIDS are not unusual problems. Some students work for hours after school, and even take time off from school to work, because they have to help their families. Others go right home to shop and cook and clean for younger siblings or ill relatives, or to negotiate a non-English speaking parent through the world. Many of our children carry a load of responsibility that seems too heavy for such young shoulders.

Every teacher is on suicide watch. Veronica didn't come home last night, do we know where she is? Jamel's father beat him again. Raquel is crying and won't tell anyone what's wrong. Calvin's mother didn't feed him, can he have an extra breakfast? Andre is high. Wendy is having an asthma attack; we need to call an ambulance. Do those look like bruises on Shirley's face?

School functions as a safe place for our children, with its structure and regularity, but it is also a controlled and controlling place, where curriculum and governance are determined without their say. They are reluctant writers. Many of them have failed in the official school discourses of subject area writing and English themes, or they have been provided with inappropriate and outworn models. Getting some of my students just to put pen to paper can take months when the usual reward systems of middle-class life simply do not apply.

My students have their own lives, full and demanding ones, that they do not necessarily check at the schoolhouse door. When they are presented with an opportunity to bring those lives into the classroom in ways that are meaningful to them, they use it.

I always plan several periods in my English class as the writing workshop. I see it so clearly: children writing quietly, drafting and revising their work; others sharing in small conferences; all of us coming together at the end for a group read. Mini-lessons and our reading will serve as appropriate genre models. Occasional pieces can be private, but most pieces will be shared. I'll note, "Please keep that in mind as you write."

I lay out this plan to them and then the questions begin:

Can I use curses?
Can I write about somebody in the class or teachers?
Can I write a letter to my mother in Ecuador?
Can I write something and not let anybody read it?
Do you swear that nobody else can go in our folders?

Well, uh, yes.

For some of my students, this is unparalleled freedom in a classroom, and they immediately begin to use it for their own purposes. They ignore the structure I would like to see in place; substitute their own idiosyncratic conventions; and work out their own agendas, which have no relation to what they're supposed to do in school. The first time a student rushes in on a reading day and says, "Can I write now? It's really important" the schedule goes, too. One rule that does remain is that I read almost everything. That's my job as the teacher, I explain, and necessary for assessment and evaluation (we negotiate the criteria later). Students learn to trust, and they usually enjoy conferences with me. They like the notice of their work and that they have their teacher's undivided attention. They may or may not follow my suggestions for revision, depending on the intention of the piece.

Students begin writing to, for, and about each other. Personal relations become a major subject. Noel, an eighth grader who divides his time between his father in Greece and his mother in New York, is in love with the school diva, the beautiful Crystal. He uses several writing periods to draft, share, revise, and edit a letter to her. He shares the draft with his closest friends, and the process of writing becomes part of the social dynamic as one friend tells another, "Noel is writing a letter to Crystal." What will it say? How will she respond? Who else will get to read it?

Noel and Crystal had gone together briefly, and now Noel is reacting to rumors of Crystal's interest in another boy. In his letter, Noel acknowledges that "acting like a kid" made him lose her, but he has learned from his mistake. It may have been the most important lesson Noel learned that week.

Crystal, from all reports, is pleased with the letter, and since Noel is an ace basketball player as well as a writer, love letters become an acceptable genre for boys as well as girls.

Priscilla, the seventh-grade diva-in-waiting, is the object of quite a different kind of letter after she writes to Hector to announce their break-up. Hector's letter is a joint effort with Calvin, one of the best writers in the class. Hector tells me that he is writing because Priscilla wants a response to her letter. "Calvin and I worked on it together," Hector says. "We thought it was a good time to do it because you said, 'Write what's on your mind.' We discussed it before, because it was how I really felt. We wrote the first draft and a second to make it neat."

I am pleased to see that writing has become a significant part of the class culture. After the nasty names he calls her in the letter, as his final insult Hector accuses Priscilla of having her friends write her letter because "I know you can't write like that. . . ."

This letter becomes the talk of the room for several periods. Students are already taking sides, and Hector and Calvin had made sure everyone knew what they were doing while they worked on the letter. When the letter is presented to Priscilla in the hallway by a friend, a planned public event, she crumples it without reading it and throws it in the garbage. "Tell him I'm not interested in anything he has to say," she tells her girlfriends.

Hector has never spent as much time and effort on any writing during the year. But the letter becomes an important part of his social discourse because he has both the opportunity and the reason to write it, and its significance obviously is not lost on Priscilla.

Students use writing time to discharge anger that is too personal or inappropriate for public expression. When Luz, a moody eighth grader, is laughed at for misreading a word, she refuses to read aloud anymore, puts her head down, and begins writing furiously in her notebook.

She hates "this stupid class," and says it's not her fault that she's a "slow reader." She's mad at her classmates and calls them names and writes that they think they're better than anyone "just because they read faster than me."

I read Luz's piece over her shoulder while she is writing, and I ask her later, when she is calmer, why she dealt with the situation by writing rather than by acting out, her usual response to stress. She says, "I wanted to leave, and I wanted to hit Calvin. I wanted to put them in their place. Writing was the fastest way to get the anger out." Of course, it wasn't, but her reasoning reveals a developing sense of herself as part of a community and an evaluation of the possible consequences of her behavior. She adds, "I wanted to storm out of the room, but it would make people talk more. If I had a fight or argument, it would make me more upset. Writing is the way I want to express myself without making a show." Luz, in retrospect, seems pleased with herself for having found a way to deal with her feelings constructively, and she continues to use writing time in class to explore her often troubled relationships with friends and family.

Students like Luz seem to enjoy using what they called "curses" or "file language." (*File,* I think, comes from a combination of *foul* and *vile,* both standard parent/teacher expressions for language that many of us find offensive.) I can see that it empowers students in some way to use language in their writing that has no place in the official school discourses.

Although I have occasional complaints about this policy, it always seems to me arbitrary and hypocritical to deny students use of the same words they hear in movies, on prime-time television in their own homes, and on the street constantly, and that they use in their own spoken language. This becomes one more part of their real lives that they must leave at the schoolhouse door, but language is not the same as a box cutter, beeper, baseball cap, or gum.

We discuss both the effectiveness and the limitations of such language and the situations where it would and would not be appropriate. Of course, not every student uses it in every piece; it remains an option of expressive language in certain modes of writing and for particular purposes, just as it is for real writers and real people.

Our school has no budget line for a guidance counselor, and family problems frequently work their way into students' writing. David, a tiny, furious boy whose mother is rumored in the neighborhood to be a *bruja*, writes a very strong poem in the desperate, angry voice of a child who finds his mother dead. He tells me, "I heard on the news that somebody was murdered, and the first three lines just popped into my head. I just continued it because it made sense." David shows it to one friend, "because I wanted him to tell me if it was good," but the smirk on his face suggested that he is not unaware of his poem's shock value. I ask David if he will share his poem with anyone else. He says he will show it to the school's director, a frequent family mediator, "because she might be interested." I cannot help thinking that David's piece is a way of telling us that something is wrong and he needs help. It is not simply a classroom exercise in poetic form.

Students also negotiate complex problems of sexual identity in their writing by using different points of view. Delia and Joann, best friends with a shared history of sexual abuse, write a series of fictional letters to each other (what their high school teacher will call an epistolary story) as lesbian lovers. The letters cover the span of two years, and after the accusations and recriminations, the former lovers reconcile as friends.

This project is a secret. The girls work by themselves and share their drafts only with me. I know I am supposed to be shocked, but since I have always included a selection of positive gay and lesbian adolescent novels in the class library, I am only a little surprised. When I ask, as I always do, why they wrote the piece, they say that they wanted to see what it felt like to be lesbians and this was a way to do it. They will not discuss it further.

All of this expressive writing is fine, colleagues allow, but what are students learning? I think that they are learning a lot, but very little of it shows up on standardized tests (except for the State Preliminary Competency Test in Writing, which we treat as a set of writing tasks, each with its own rules and conventions, performed for a particular audience and political purpose; they do very well on that). The primary work of adolescence is becoming a person—negotiating an identity between the self and the community. Students know this and are actively engaged in the process every waking moment. School, with its institutional purpose of socialization into a community of shared knowledge and represented experience—and its lack of opportunity for individual decision making—can become peripheral to what a student perceives as her real life.

Young people need to understand their place in the world. They need to reflect on and imagine their own lives. This is the hidden agenda that they all bring into the classroom. They can be supported in using school structures to accomplish this task of understanding.

Students want to do well if they have a real purpose. When they decide that a piece of writing is important to them, for a myriad of private and public reasons, they work until the writing does what they want it or need it to do. In the process, they experiment with form, refer to genre models, consider audience, discuss with peers, draft, revise, and selectively share their work. They often require privacy, as we all do, and I allow it. I do not always agree with their intentions or effects, and not everything is permitted, but their choices are respected.

I sometimes wish we could put together a school publication with clever poems and nice stories that the Parents' Association and the district office would applaud. But my students have a different vision of what writing is for. By showing me how school can be a place to realize that vision, they have transformed mine.

Bibliography

Dyson, A. H. 1994. "Confronting the Split Between 'The Child' and Children: Toward New Curricular Visions of the Child Writer." *English Education* 26 (1): 12–28.

✳ *The Boy in the Bulls Basketball Shirt*

Mike McCormick

When the classroom teacher barks the name
of the boy who needs to go
to the Title One room
to finish his book,

Maurice furrows his brow
and scowls like a player
who's been tossed from the game
for a flagrant foul.

"Ain't no way I'm reading that trash."

In my room
he slams the book
on the hardwood table,

flops down on a folding chair,

crosses his arms
and glares
dead ahead.

I sidle to the table
and unfold the sports page,
"Let's see how many Michael got last night."

Together we skim the line score.
"45 points!" Maurice calls
and as he dives in for more

I step to the sidelines
and feel an ovation rise
in my heart

because Maurice
is checking back
into the game.

Rocking Their Way to Literacy
ESL Adolescents Strengthen Their Love of Reading

Gerardine Cannon

My students, who number ninety this year, come from many countries around the world and speak a total of seventeen different languages. Some arrive in the United States academically prepared and only need to learn English. Others have no formal education or have progressed no further than the second or third grade. The last group are the most difficult to teach. They have never learned to read in their native languages and, therefore, have no literacy skills to transfer. Though the challenge is great, I thrive on meeting it. Some of my greatest joys are watching young teenagers become fluent readers.

Helping teenagers become comfortable enough with literacy to develop lifelong reading habits is a daunting task. At this point in their young lives, other habits have already taken hold: a dislike for "reading"; an association of reading with skills lessons; a belief that they are incapable of reading "hard" books; a need to be a teenager, not a student. It's not easy being an adolescent and knowing you have two years in which you must learn enough literacy skills to function at the high school level.

Developing reading fluency is a gradual process for ESL students, just as it is for mainstream readers. Unless they are allowed the time necessary to become comfortable with literacy, they will become bi-illiterate, unable to read well in either English or their native languages. If these students are to complete high school and perhaps pursue a postsecondary education, they must become literate by the end of the eighth grade, honing the skills necessary to read one-, two-, and three-hundred-page novels in their high school literature classes. It must be remembered that these students are already fourteen or fifteen years old. They will either develop their reading skills now or they will remain static.

These students need at least two years of concentrated reading time to become proficient readers who are close to meeting the expectations for their grade levels. Most need more. There can be only so much phonics, so much round robin reading, so much identifying the main idea. At some point they have to become absorbed in a story. They have to stop their minds from wandering. They have to sit alone and read.

Real Books for Real Readers

For the past few years I have avoided saying, "I teach reading." After years of exposing my students to language experience techniques and functional reading exercises involving bus schedules and baseball cards, I realized that although I was teaching reading "skills" and my students were learning reading "skills," *I was a "reader" and they weren't.* It became evident that in spite of all the methods, strategies, and theories, successful reading ultimately comes when the students pick up books and read. The only way my ESL students would become readers was to read.

What incited me to change was a research paper I read titled "How to Teach Reading to ESL Students." There was a section on phonics and final consonants: FI*B*, SO*B*, DA*B*, CRI*B*. Yet many ESL students don't even understand the meaning of most of those words! There was a section on language experience. There was one on functional reading: street signs, labels, maps, application forms, telephone directories. Then there was physical response reading: Stand up! Sit down! This was reading? How about Dialogues! Interviews! Sight Words! Word Families: A-N-D, h*and,* s*and,* l*and,* gr*and.* And so on. Here were great strategies for beginning literacy, but what about reading BOOKS? Nowhere in the article did it suggest that students read a book.

And so I tucked all those strategies away: the dialogues, the interviews, the word families, the bus schedules. (I tucked them away, but not too far away, for I have learned in my many years of teaching that nothing ever completely loses its value.) Instead, I declared that my ESL students would read only "good" (adolescent) literature.

At that time, I didn't understand that although "good" literature has its place in a reading classroom, it is not the only—or even the most—appropriate reading material for many of my students. Young adult literature requires a concentration that can thwart the flow necessary for the development of fluency. For most of my students, reading "good" literature is analogous to translating a foreign language. They struggle with the vocabulary, the grammar, the syntactical complexity. During this struggle, they lose the beauty of the language, the sense of the story, the relationship among the characters. Their frustration is almost palpable. Adolescent literature is best addressed in a context where there is maximum support from teacher and classmates, where there is more formal attention to the needs of the readers. When students are trying to develop fluency in reading, the only "good" literature is the literature they are able and willing to read.

To help students develop the love of reading that would catapult them into the world of literacy, I introduced Curious George, The Berenstain Bears, The Baby-Sitters Little Sister, the Fear Street Series, R. L. Stine, Judy Blume, Ann M. Martin, and Walter Dean Myers. Out came the innovative and unorthodox literacy practices I had been learning about in all those workshops, conferences, and panel discussions I had been attending. I am grateful to my school district for trusting my professional judgment when I asked for the time to pursue such training sessions. So much of what I am is a direct result of all those experiences.

A Comfortable Classroom

I am convinced that the more comfortable these educationally needy students are, the more receptive they are to assuming the task of learning to read. Five years ago I brought rocking chairs into my classroom (Figure 1). My reading classes haven't been the same since.

> Having a rocking chair in Room 24 is like being back in Puerto Rico with my great-grandmother and great-grandpa listening to their stories.
>
> Luis

I think Ms. Cannon did a good job to put the rocking chairs in Room 24 because when we read we feel good and we relax. I hope she gets twenty rocking chairs because I don't like it when I don't have a turn.

Benvinda

Having a rocking chair in Room 24 means no back problems.

Carlos

Well, as for me, I love rocking chairs. We all sit down when Ms. Cannon is reading a book. Each person gets to sit in one when it's their turn. Sometimes we have to take a pillow but inside our hearts we all want Ms. Cannon's rocking chairs.

Jose

Rocking chairs make reading voluntary rather than a job.

Sergio

Having a rocking chair helps us put something that we're reading in our heads.

Candida

I think it's great to have rocking chairs in Room 24 because you get a nice book and sit and relax and read. It would be great to have a lot of rocking chairs so each student could sit on one and read a book or maybe even just sit quietly and think of wonderful things.

Lucia

Figure 1. *Graphics Illustrator: German Cardona. Grade 8. Jenks Junior High School. Pawtucket, Rhode Island.*

Having a rocking chair in Room 24 means that you have something to sit on and read and while you're at it you can rock yourself and enjoy the ride. To me having a rocking chair is the best thing that can happen to a reading class.

Aida

The comforts-of-home strategy started the day I dragged a one-armed, abandoned rocking chair across the hall into my rather unconventional reading classroom. I already had a dozen or so pillows that my students would use to stretch out under desks, in corners, behind cabinets. Now I had a rocking chair! The first few weeks I hogged it for myself during the read-aloud portion of each class period, but then the begging started, and I had to develop a list of rocking chair "candidates." My students loved sitting on that dilapidated old rocker so much that I have since added seven others. My goal is to have a rocking chair for each student. Since my largest class consists of twenty-three students I am barely on my way—but the word is out!

Pillows and rocking chairs now vie for space with the desks and chairs. Quiet fills the once noisy classroom. I have created an atmosphere that few of my students have ever enjoyed before. Though some have rocking chairs at home, most have never had the joy of sitting in one with a favorite book. Literacy has not been a meaningful part of their life experience. For the majority of my students, the only reading material available at home is the bills and flyers that drop through the mail slot each day. For most, there has never been a bedtime rock with a parent and *The Three Bears*. No rainy day curl-up on the couch with Ramona or the Hardy Boys. This is their chance.

Finding Materials

For twenty minutes every day, each of my eight junior high school reading classes has the task of finding books, reading them, and writing about them in their journals. In those first few years, this was a real challenge. The school library was stocked with junior high school reading material far beyond my ESL students' independent reading levels.

I turned homeward to my own bookshelves, which were loaded with Golden books and fairy tales that my two daughters, Gerra and Kate, had long outgrown. However, I was hesitant to fill the shelves of my seventh-

and eighth-grade reading classes with books that my daughters had read in early elementary school. I feared my students would be offended. I needn't have worried. They were soon clamoring for more *Cinderella, Bambi,* and *The Little Engine That Could.*

Because literature had never been a part of their childhoods, my students were enthralled with this new world of stories and characters. It was a joy to watch them settle in with Pinocchio and Amelia Bedelia. And since they loved these stories, I began to haunt used bookstores for the twenty-five cent bargain. School fairs and garage and tag sales provided another great source for material. I tried to find books with universal themes: humor, animals, horror, love, friendship, and sports.

My "library" now contains some two thousand books. *Curious George Takes a Job* and *The Baby-Sitters Little Sister* sit side by side with young adult novels such as *It's Not the End of the World* and *The Giver.* Students have access to books that they are capable of reading independently—books they will chose and read of their own volition during the two years that they spend with me.

Year One: Laying the Foundation

Most of the students in my ESL classroom are two to six grade levels behind their American counterparts in reading. During their first year with me, many are incapable of selecting a book and sitting down to read quietly for twenty minutes. Few, if any, have ever written in a journal or completed reading a novel.

For them, "reading" is limited to looking at the illustrations; mindlessly turning pages; putting the book back after a ten-minute scan; glancing around the room; being easily distracted by a cough, a door opening, a chair moving; talking; walking; visiting the bookcase. They can read words, sentences, and paragraphs without grasping the meaning of the text. They can blithely ignore crucial vocabulary. They can begin a new chapter with total disregard as to what preceded it.

They think of themselves not as readers but as page flippers, picture scanners, school attendees—not students. Because they need time to acquire literacy in English, their first year with me is spent becoming familiar and comfortable with books. They learn how to judge books by their covers; they learn to remember a storyline from one day to the next;

they learn to sit quietly with a book in hand; they learn how to write about books in their journals. Assuming this task of learning to read is a huge undertaking. Many are still struggling at the end of their first year.

Year Two: Building the Reader

From September to January of the second year, I revive habits so painstakingly developed during the previous year, reinforce metacognitive skills, and continue nurturing my students. At this point, many of them are beginning to think of themselves as readers, although they are still somewhat dependent on illustrations. It is time to move forward to nonillustrated or sparsely illustrated books—a potentially traumatic experience that my students think they will never be able to accomplish or enjoy! Fear and uncertainty shadow their faces as they pick up longer books and scan page after page of uninterrupted print. This step requires that my students take a leap of faith. Their reading proficiency is approaching fluency and only sustained practice at an independent level will result in sustained success. This is the time when they must make a vested interest. This is the time for a commitment.

Hopefully, the habits and skills that we have nurtured so carefully over the past months will now emerge and carry the readers through this most difficult phase. They are now able to knowledgeably scan the shelves for reading material. They can use their familiarity with authors and genres to make choices for independent reading. They are comfortable asking classmates and me for recommendations. They have begun to appreciate the elements of plot, tone, style, and characterization. Everything is in place for them to read more challenging books: They just don't know they can do it.

But I know they can. Their classroom behavior has become more refined: They can now sit and read quietly for twenty minutes at a time; they more quickly become absorbed in stories; they have increased their powers of concentration and learned to ignore common distractions; they seek quiet places away from talkative friends; and, even better for me, they groan when the bell rings to change classes. Their self-perception has improved. They are aware of their own literacy. They assume the role of the serious reader. They take control of their own education.

This is not to say there are no lapses. From time to time there is a regression to *The Berenstain Bears,* but it is only temporary. They find little but a sentimental satisfaction on that level now. This part of their reading experience is over. They may enjoy those books once again in years to come when they read to their own children, but for now they are finally ensconced in the world of young adult literature.

The Book Presentation

By the middle of the second year, my ESL students are reading and writing well enough to use their skills in new ways. One of the most effective is the book presentation. Sitting in a rocking chair in the front of the room, students talk to their classmates about books they have enjoyed. Using guidelines I have developed, they discuss the author, the plot, the characters, their opinions, and their recommendations. They explain the cover illustration and read a passage from the book. Then they answer questions from their classmates: the audience. This process is particularly helpful for ESL students because it addresses all four areas of language development: reading, writing, listening, and speaking. It also involves higher cognitive functions such as evaluating, synthesizing, and analyzing.

Keeping the remaining students focused on the presenter was a challenge until I developed the Audience Participation Form (Figure 2), which students complete during and after the presentation. The four sections are designed to keep students listening and thinking throughout the entire presentation so they can formulate intelligent comments and questions for the follow-up discussion. In order to ensure full participation during this phase, I give credit for their contributions. Both quantity and quality count.

My Role

It is my professional responsibility to provide the opportunity, the skills, the atmosphere, the materials (including the rocking chairs!) for my students to develop the reading and writing skills that will underlie their literacy. I have control over many areas of my classroom. I display my own love of reading and writing. I bring the world of literature, authors, and illustrators into my students' lives. I provide the classroom library, the pil-

AUDIENCE PARTICIPATION FORM

Your name_____

Presenter's name_____

Book title_____

Author_____

Date_____

1. What part of the presentation did you like the best? In one or two sentences explain why you chose that part.

2. Write two questions about the presentation, the book, and/or the author.

    A.

    B.

3. Would you like to read this book? Yes____ No____ In one or two sentences give reasons for your decision.

4. What does this book remind you of? It could be a personal experience, an experience of friends or family, a movie, a TV program, a book, etc. Write your thoughts in two or three sentences.

Figure 2. *Audience Participation Form*

lows, the comfortable furniture, the quiet. I unearth the native intelligence lying dormant beneath family problems, poor self-esteem, and uneven educational experiences. I try to convince my students of the importance of reading and writing in their own lives. What I cannot do, however, is make my students *want* to read and write. That is something they must accept responsibility for. To my delight, most of them do.

Bibliography

Blume, Judy. 1972. *It's Not the End of the World.* New York: Bantam Books.

Delamare, David. 1993. *Cinderella.* New York: Green Tyger Press.

Lowry, Lois. 1993. *The Giver.* New York: Laurel Leaf.

Martin, Ann M. 1990. *The Baby-Sitters Little Sister.* New York: Scholastic Inc.

Salten, Felix. 1984. *Bambi.* Racine: Western Publishing Co. Inc.

Piper, Watty. 1990. *The Little Engine That Could.* New York: Platt & Munk.

Rey, L. A. 1947. *Curious George Takes a Job.* Boston: Houghton Mifflin Company.

Time to Heal
One Student, One Paper, One Story

Jane A. Kearns

Kris walked into my class crying. It was the end of October, and she was transferring into the class. My freshmen were at the end of a writing unit, at the place where a hundred different things happen every ten minutes, and I was spinning plates as deftly and quickly and professionally as possible. These so-called low-level students had taken to writing; though they struggled to develop their information, they loved the idea that they could write about whatever interested them.

Where was Kris to fit in? Why was she transferring from another class now? How could I get her to understand what was going on today?

I took the sobbing Kris to an empty seat and asked her if I could help. When she shook her head, I gave her a folder filled with a variety of blank paper, then wrote her name in calligraphy on the tab. "Kris, we are all working on our writing. You can write on any subject you want," I told her, " but it should be something you know about."

In between sobs and shakes, she whispered, "My cat." I didn't have the heart to tell her that normally cats were taboo, a no-no subject in my class. ("Allergies, you know.") I just nodded and continued my appointed conferencing rounds.

I asked Carolyn, a quiet, thoughtful girl, if she knew Kris. "I think she lives in my neighborhood," she replied.

"Go see if she is all right," I said. "See if there is anything you can do to welcome her. Explain what we do with our writing program, too."

Kris told Carolyn that she had been thrown out of another class; the teacher picked on her, teased her, insulted her in front of the other students. When Kris spoke back, the teacher tossed her out and had her transferred. (The same person, who has since left teaching, was a bully in the teachers' room, too, where she would torment new staff and unwitting substitutes.)

"I told her she was safe here," Carolyn said to me. "I told her you're OK."

"Thanks."

"Did you know she's writing about her cat? I didn't tell her not to."

"That's fine. I couldn't tell her either. Please check on her again during class if you have a chance. I will too."

During the busy class, I forgot about Kris. After the bell rang I showed her where we stored our folders. "How did you do?" I asked, expecting a single paragraph on her cat.

She handed me sheet after sheet, six long pages of everything she could remember about her cat. I mentally sneezed.

"Would you read this?" she asked.

That night I read her story, sentence after sentence, line after line—no cohesion, no focus, just cat:

> My cat was a Tigar. Her name was Fig. My brother gave her to me. The first night we had her she slept under the covers with me. She like to play in the snow with me. When I would go out to go sliding she would come and get in the sled with me and go down the hill. . . .

As with all the students, I spoke to Kris the next day before class and handed her a written note about the paper: *You certainly know a lot about your cat. Writers need to be observant and you are. Good title, My Tiger.*

Soon Kris moved her seat next to her new friend. (I have an open seating plan: as long as students produce, they can sit wherever they want.) These two freshmen girls became the most electric conference partners and process writers I ever had. They worked at their writing, loved to help each other, knew they had a chance to succeed, relaxed in the freedom of the class, and relished both our quiet times and talk times. They felt safe in the rhythm of the room and the cadence of the composing process.

On my class sheet, I noted Kris's work and wrote a reminder to teach her how to cut and paste, a technique for topic development that involved reordering for emphasis. I had not taught this strategy to this class as a whole because every other student still grappled to complete two or three paragraphs where Kris started out with six pages.

In a writing conference with Kris, I told her that sometimes even though we can place all of our information down on paper, our thoughts are not as organized, clear, and direct as our writing needs to be. One strategy is to cut and paste the sentences and graphs to rearrange the thoughts while still keeping the gist of the piece.

Once she had cut and pasted, it became her favorite revising technique. She loved the physicalness of the scissors, the tangible activity that allowed her to redefine her information into a more interesting piece. Kris willingly introduced cutting and pasting to others in the class. This role of teacher enabled Kris to regain some pride and control of her school days.

Over the next few weeks and months, Kris also became an active participant in our reading and responding, talking and writing—but still she often cried or looked like she had been crying. When I asked if I could help, she'd say no and quietly go about her work.

The class accepted this behavior. I assumed this was because they knew more of her background than I did. They never hurt her feelings or teased about her crying.

One spring day, when Kris was crying uncontrollably, Carolyn told me it was because Kris had just broken up with her boyfriend. "Kris," I asked, "Can I help?"

"No, Ms. Kearns. I'm going to write about it."

Kris, I had learned, loved the activity of the writing process, the listing, the tries at leads, the cutting and pasting, the numbering of sections to be rearranged. She wrote the date every time she revised. Her papers still rambled, but she worked hard and helped others improve their papers. She became a popular and proficient peer reader. After this particular crying spell, she brainstormed everything she knew about her boyfriend Bobby.

Soon I learned that this was really love from afar. They had never dated and really only spoke in the corridors. The day that they *broke up*, Kris had approached Bobby in the cafeteria to start a conversation. Verbally he shoved her away. More rejection! And more tears.

Her list about Bobby included more than fifty items. When she came to write, however, the piece rambled in a sort of freshman-*all-about*, a form common in primary grades. It was not surprising that she had no central focus; she really didn't know her subject. She wasn't writing about what she really knew—a theme I had preached all year.

The next day, more tears. When she met with a small group of students for a peer conference, the conversation turned to how easily she cries. "I've cried a lot," she told the others.

"Why not write about that?" Carolyn offered.

A firm believer in the power of process, Kris spent the rest of that period listing titles for the new proposed piece on crying, something she did know much about:

My new bike
Falling Skinned Knees
Gary
Crying A lot
My boyfriend

This strategy of listing titles before, during, and sometimes after writing gave these students a sense of accomplishment and focus. At the same time, it provided them with an alternative to writing numerous composition pages each writing day, a task that frightened and dissuaded them. The psychology of writing shorter lines gave these students the power and control to be writers.

Kris looked over her titles list and selected "Crying A lot." She centered the title and wrote her name and the date at the top of the paper, a ritual that gave students a sense of authority and command. Then she began writing.

"When I was five . . . when I was seven . . . when I was nine . . . ten . . . eleven. . . ." On and on she roamed, exploring friends and family and relationships. For three days she worked on her crying piece. When she returned after being out a week, she picked it up without losing the tempo. For another four days, Kris recounted every memory she had of crying. With her conference partners, she talked about the focus of the paper. They asked insightful questions.

"Do you need to write about every year?"

"Which times were most important?"

"What was the worst time?"

With the writing center scissors, Kris cut and pasted, sharpening her thoughts and her focus. She removed the excess and cut her paper down to a lean three pages.

After rearranging this version, she told me she had a better idea for her paper. Then she started a new list of titles, trying to hone in on a better title with a clearer focus:

When I was little
Crying A lot
Hard Times
It takes Time to heel
Broken Heart

At the top of the revised version of her story, she crossed out her old title and wrote her new one: "It takes Time to heel." I told her there was no need to recopy the cut-and-pasted piece, one of the most boring and insignificant activities we used to mistake for real writing. She signed her name on the board, noting she wanted a peer conference. When her partners reached a stopping point, Kris read her revised and newly focused piece. After Kris added one piece of information they thought she needed, they approved. She then presented her almost-finished paper to three peer editors to check. Kris now had her paper.

It Takes Time to Heal

When I was five and skinned my knees from falling, all it took was for my mom or dad to wash it, kiss it and put a band aid on it, then a hug to go with it. The band aid was the best part because I could show it off to all my friends.

But when I was 7 and just got my new bike, my brother Gary who was bigger than me and older too, wanted to ride it. He made me let him ride it. He was just turning a corner and my brand new bike busted in two because he was too big for it. Right then I started crying my eyes out. Then my parents drove up. What's wrong? they asked.

"Gary busted my bike." I said. My parents were so mad they made him give me his bike till he could get another one. (Well, I never did get a new bike from my brother.)

I remember once when I was 10 years old, my parents were going away for a week. They told me I had to go to my aunt and uncle's house. I really didn't like going there because it was way up in the country. In the summer there were billions of bugs that eat you alive. There were no stores around for miles from my aunt and uncle's house. And my uncle had the car all day.

But when it came time to go to my aunt and uncle's, I started crying saying, "I don't want to go." I wanted to stay with my brothers Matt and Gary. My brother Matt was 20 and Gary was 17 years old. My parents didn't have time to fight with me.

"Let her stay," my father said. My brother said "yes." I got to go bike riding with them, and play baseball. I had the time of my life that week. I really felt like I was important that week because all their friends really liked having me around. I think they did because they showed it by taking me swimming and for pizza.

Well, I'm not a little girl any more. I'm 15 years old. I have a lot more problems and decisions than when I was 5, 7 and 10.

A broken heart take more than a kiss and a hug to heal. It takes time and lots of love from someone you are close to. When my boyfriend and I broke up I couldn't eat or sleep. I was depressed all the time. All I did was cry.

I guess a broken heart is like a skinned knee because they both take time to heal. I don't skin my knees anymore but I will find someone else to love.

In June, analyzing her own writing, Kris wrote:

My writing needs more revising and I feel the more writing I did the better I got—but it still needs more revising.

When you write a comp, I think the hardest part is trying to find an opening sentence but then once I start writing it's all right. Also when writing a comp, you want the title to surprise, so when you first look at the title you don't know what it is about. When I write I try to be descriptive and humorous, no one wants to read a boring paper.

Our class environment, I believe, gave Kris and her friends the dignity that, over the years, slowly had been taken from them. The rest of the class were students much like her, unobtrusive, suspicious of school, below average in grades—the underside of school. The shadows. Their inability to manage grammar and the traditional exercises that we teachers used to see as learning made them failures. Kris and the other students needed to use a process that was hands-on, needed to feel accepted, needed to know people were listening. They needed school to be a safe harbor, a predictable place where they could succeed. They needed time to work at their own pace, to find a voice for their experiences and memories, to become writers.

Sadly, Kris dropped out the following year. So did I really meet the challenge? Or just add another Band-Aid?

I often tell teachers in writing and reading process or portfolio workshops that as teachers we need to spend every minute of our teaching day searching for teaching moments. We cannot know what our students will be or what they will do, so we must not waste a moment. I tell these teachers, "Don't worry if the teacher next year doesn't teach process. Students will gain much from experiencing *your* process class of freedom and discipline and success."

I say this and I mean it—but when I think of Kris, I wonder if I did enough. Did her writing success in this class help her with adult issues? I like to think it did; as a teacher I *need* to believe it did.

 *Mariano*

Robert Roth

"Wassup, dude?" I turned around and saw a big, round kid with a shaved head and prominent ears standing outside my classroom door. "Gotta go now, but I'll catch you later!" He flashed a broad smile and lumbered down the hall, his overalls sagging. A few seconds later, I heard his voice loud and clear from the hallway. "Fuck you, bitch!" That was the first time I met Mariano.

We really got to know each other during hallsweep. Hallsweep is an institution at our middle school. Teachers walk assigned routes at the beginning of their prep period, searching the halls for students who haven't gotten to class on time. You track down the offenders, walk them to the second floor, and line them up against a wall near the stairwell while security guards take down their names and homerooms and assign them to detention.

Mariano had mastered hallsweep. Walking well behind the teacher who "caught" him, he'd run his hands over every single locker, mumbling barely audible obscenities the whole time. As he passed an open classroom, he'd poke his head in, wave at bored students, and create a minor scene. At the second floor lineup, he'd tell the security guards to stop lecturing him and hum songs to himself while they tried. Sharp, intelligent, witty, he could give as good as he got. You caught your breath when you ran into him on your shift.

During our many hallsweep encounters, we developed a bit of a friendship. Walking with me instead of ten feet behind, he started talking about which teachers he hated, how rotten the school was, what fights he'd had that day. When the year ended, he pulled me aside and asked me to request him for my seventh-grade class the next year.

No way was I going to request Mariano. It was one thing to be his hallsweep pal, quite another to teach him world history for ten months. As it turned out, I didn't get him in any of my seventh-grade classes that year, nor did I see him as much on hallsweep. But I did hear about frequent referrals, periodic fights with other students, run-ins with the principal and assistant principal. Mariano lived close to the edge, always one step away from an expulsion, one incident away from a police report.

I don't know how he made it through the seventh grade. But when I looked through my eighth-grade list at the beginning of the next year, there he was. I can't say I was overjoyed to see his name, but I took it as a challenge.

Mariano started off the year enthusiastically, plunking himself down in the first row, his new, crisp Pendleton buttoned to the top. He missed a few homework assignments, came late a few times, forgot his materials. But he was right there—engaged, alive, inquisitive. His questions were never easily answered: "Why didn't the Indians just kill Columbus?" "Why didn't the Africans come together and stop slavery?" "Why are people prejudiced toward other races?" "If the first human beings began in Africa, why aren't we all black?" In spite of his studied attempts to maintain distance, he had a stake in the class and in his performance.

Mariano also loved the school's new computer lab. Spending all his spare time there—at lunch, before school, after school—he steadily improved his computer skills. Down in the office the talk started to change. "Have you noticed how Mariano's matured this year?" "It's so great that he's into computers." "Maybe he'll graduate!"

It didn't last. Mariano began to fade around December. It seemed like the day-to-day work just got to be too much. He kept forgetting his assignments, falling behind, missing class. There were a few flare-ups, mostly with other students. He really went after LaTonya, tripping her as she passed by his desk, barking like a dog when she spoke up in class. Nasty stuff. I started pulling him outside for little chats, letting him know he'd crossed my line. His resentment built and he stopped doing his homework. Classroom discussions no longer interested him. Other teachers came by to tell me how impossible he was in their classes. When I heard him mutter "Fuck you" as I passed by his desk one day, I knew I had a big problem as well.

I kept him after class and asked him for a list of his complaints. Why was he so pissed off? Why the attitude? He started to talk—about how boring school was, about how everyone, including me, singled him out. Other people made fun of LaTonya, but I didn't get on their case. Other people didn't bring in their homework, but I let it slide. Oh yeah, and when were we going to study Mexican history? He'd been in school for years and never learned anything about his people, his race. Why weren't there any Latino teachers? How come so many teachers—like me—were white? How come there was a student assembly for Black History Month, but nothing for Cinco de Mayo? How did I expect him to do so much homework, anyway?

It was a long list. I searched for common ground. Yes, he had a point about Mexican history. And he was absolutely right about the need for Latino teachers. But we were just about to begin a unit on Mexico, the Mexican War, immigration, Latinos/as in the United States. Could he help? Could he work with me to figure out what we should study? Did he know anyone who could help us get resources and ideas together?

Excitement flashed across his face. His dad knew everything about Latino history. Everything. He was an expert. I asked if he could come to school and meet with us, if we could work on this unit together.

The conversation stopped. His toughness melted away, and he just sat there shaking his head and tapping his fingers. It was impossible for his father to come, he told me, because he'd had a serious heart attack. Then he paused, trying to compose himself. I reached out to touch his arm and he tensed, but he let my hand rest there. After a while he began to talk about how scared he was, how hard it was to concentrate. Then he just got up, said "Thanks," and walked out the door.

That was our last conversation about his father. I raised the subject a couple of times, but he always said everything was fine. I asked about it in the office and was told that Mariano was receiving counseling from the school psychologist. When we did the unit on Mexico, he came alive again for a while. Sitting straight up, his eyes focused, he had information to impart. Did we all realize that this classroom was on land stolen from Mexico? Did we know the story of the young Mexican cadets who jumped to their deaths rather than surrender during the Mexican-American War? And how could Mexicans be considered "illegal" immigrants when this was their land?

More engaged now, Mariano's attendance improved and his homework started coming in more regularly. But he still couldn't bring himself to do the final research paper, even though his chosen topic was Pancho Villa. When he finally turned in his report, it was two weeks late and totally copied from a book.

He got a C in my class but ended up with seven U's and three F's for the year, way beyond the school limit for participating in graduation ceremonies. His anger seemed to grow as the year moved on. Over the final weeks, he was suspended three times, once for defying a teacher and twice for fighting.

The explosion finally came right before the end of the school year. Mariano got into a taunting back-and-forth with another eighth grader in the hallway. Before anyone could intervene, Mariano punched the other student in the face. Blood was everywhere.

They called me into the office when Mariano's dad arrived to talk to the police. Ms. Alvarez, the student advisor, wanted me there to give Mariano support. "He'll feel better if you're in the room," she said. I wasn't sure, but I went. Head down, his voice a halting whisper, Mariano sat nervously next to his father, whose worn face spoke of weeks of illness. His father had been in that office many times before and was not happy to be there now. Preoccupied with the crisis at hand, he never even glanced my way, focusing his gaze on the head counselor who was detailing the incident. When the counselor brought out a signed statement from Mariano admitting guilt, his father blew up. How could the school get his son to sign a confession without his being there? Yes, he was concerned about the other boy, but his son had rights too. He had told the principal that he was coming right over. Couldn't they have had enough respect to wait before involving Mariano with the police? His eyes swept the room. I couldn't think of anything to say.

The other kid got some stitches at the hospital and went home later that day. No charges were filed against Mariano. Not this time. I saw him once more before the end of the semester. At school to pick up stuff from his locker, he stopped by my room to say good-bye. "Don't worry," he told me, shaking my hand. "I'll be back to visit next year."

Mariano sticks in my mind. When I think of him, I'm troubled, and I can't exorcise it. I'm forced to step back and reflect on the daunting odds so many students face. And I'm confronted with the limits of my own ability to understand, to make a difference. Sometimes at the end of a school year I find myself looking back and revising, holding on tightly to successes while shoving the pain and frustration into the recesses of memory. I don't want to do that with Mariano.

Step by Step
Learning in Many Voices

Janet Allen and Kyle E. Gonzalez

Step by step, I can't see any other way of accomplishing anything. I never looked at the consequences of missing a big shot. Why? Because when you think about the consequences you always think of a negative result.

Michael Jordan
I Can't Accept Not Trying

Kyle began her year in much the same way I had begun mine by balancing her days with time for shared reading and writing, independent literacy explorations, and developing personal relationships with the students. I helped her find her first books for reading aloud, and together we found books for her classroom library. We discussed the value of using recorded books to supplement the shared reading Kyle could fit into her two-period block. She wrote a grant that gave her the funds for portable tape players with headsets and a beginning supply of books on tape for her students to use during their independent reading. I listened and gave suggestions when she was confused and angry. Kyle's journey with J.C. represents the challenges she faced each day with these students. Fortunately, it also represents the meaningful days we spend when we help students join the "literacy club" (Smith 1988).

Kyle's Journey with J.C.

I did not meet J.C. until the third of week of school. I stopped calling his name from the role by the middle of the second week, assuming that I would have to turn it in on the "no show" list. Finally, he arrived one day, shuffling slowly into my classroom, his face sullen and tired. Although I wasn't sure I wanted one more challenge, I tried to make my welcome and introduction sincere. I knew the risk he had taken to enter the classroom after missing the beginning of school. I couldn't even hear his mumbled reply.

Eyes averted, he walked almost in slow motion to the back of the room and plopped down at one of the tables. I was reading *Scorpions* by Walter Dean Myers, the first novel we had chosen for shared reading in my combined seventh- and eighth-grade class. I handed J.C. a copy of the book and asked the class if someone could explain to him what it was about so far. Silence. Please, I thought, please, somebody, have the courage to answer the question. Finally, Donnelle raised his hand and told J.C. about Jamal, a twelve-year-old boy living in New York City. My heart soared as I listened to Donnelle, who gained confidence and momentum as he watched my smiling face. He actually seemed surprised that he was remembering what the story was about.

At this point we had been reading the book for about a week. The students *finally* seemed interested enough in the novel to stop making rude comments, whispering, and poking each other as I read to them. I hoped that J.C. might take an interest in the novel. My fear was that his lack of interest might distract those students who still only were marginally hooked on the value of books.

During the next period, however, and for the remainder of most of the first semester, J.C. simply stared into space, mouth slightly open, looking as if he were in a completely different world. His attendance was sporadic, and he began to test the boundaries not only in my class but in his other classes as well. Although he was quiet and withdrawn in my room, his behavior was *extremely* disruptive in some other classes, and so he became an all-too-familiar face in our in-school suspension program (I. S. S.). Finally, I began to realize that if I were going to reach J.C., I was going to have to do it in the in-school suspension room. Each day as I took work to him, I always found him isolated at the back corner of the stark, eerily silent room. He stared at the wall, a few worksheets scattered in front of him, no pencil or pen. Shocked at his lethargy, I glanced over at the I. S. S. instructor. Sensing my disgust at the waste of time, he was quick to place the guilt elsewhere. "I told him," the instructor practically shouted at me, "that I am tired of giving him something to write with. So if he doesn't bring a pencil, he's just going to sit there!" J.C. continued to stare at the wall, not even flinching at the anger in the teacher's voice. I left the I. S. S. room shaken by the hopelessness of both J.C.'s situation and my inability to reach him.

Sadly, my attempts at reaching J.C. when he *was* in my classroom were not working any better. He continued to vacillate between staring blankly into space or disrupting others. I began to have to ask him to leave my classroom. I tried to explain that his behavior was not appropriate. My words were usually cut off by the ominous door slam, right after J.C. stood in the doorway proclaiming in colorful language what he thought of me and the entire school. I tried to console myself that I was justified in losing J.C. in order to save the rest of the students, but I knew the marginal truth in that as I turned to receive the accusing glances from the rest of the class. They seemed to say, "You're just like all of the rest of them."

When I could let go of my anger and guilt, I realized that at least now J.C. was beginning to communicate with me. Although it certainly was not the communication I would have preferred, it certainly was effective communication. I heard his message loud and clear!

After the first of those instances, I drove home, crying and dodging cars in the city traffic. It was the first time in my twenty-four years that I had actually preferred silence to the radio. "I'm losing my mind," I told myself. "I'm never going to be able to reach these kids."

Strangely, by the next morning I was able to walk back into our classroom with renewed determination. I had to remind myself that failure is all that these students have ever encountered in school, and it would take a long time before they expected anything other than my contributing to their continued failure. That day I wrote a Here and Now (Kirby and Liner 1988) on the board:

> Tell me what you like the most and the least about school. What could you do to make school better? What could teachers do to make school better?

Most of the students began to write: Theresa with her usual vigor; Yolanda in her shy manner; Brian with amazement; and Donnelle and Malcolm with hesitation, automatically doubting their abilities. J.C., as usual, sat in the back and began taunting Donnelle, Malcolm, and John. I knew that it would surely turn into an explosion if I did not intervene soon.

"J.C., would you come and sit with me?" I asked, patting the chair beside me. He rolled his eyes. "I won't bite. I just want to talk with you for a few minutes, and I think that Malcolm and the others will be able to start writing if they separate, too."

I glanced over at them. "Man, I can't believe this junk," and other comments came from their group. Malcolm was the first to move. As Donnelle moved to a computer, I could hear him grumble, "Dog." John remained at the table but finally moved as I continued to keep my eyes locked onto his. J.C. was left alone.

Finding His Voice

J.C.'s expression clearly told me that I was the last person in the world he'd like to sit by, let alone talk with. Abruptly, he stood up. "OK, Ms. Connnnnnvict!" he announced, turning my last name of Conry into a multisyllabic word as he trotted to the front of the room. He, of course, got the laughter he was looking for. He deliberately moved the chair farther away from me and then sat down, glancing around for attention. Seeing very little, he immediately launched into his almost cathartic state.

"J.C.," I began. "How about us working on this Here and Now together?" No response. "Why don't I read it to you?" After I had finished, I looked at him expectantly. He stared at the blank computer screen. "Do you want to tell me your thoughts about this and I'll type them for you?" I offered. I often did this with students when I saw that they were having difficulty with writing. It was a way that I could prove to them that they did have thoughts that not only could be spoken, but were worth putting on paper, too. He nodded his head. I almost fell out of my chair. "OK, whenever you're ready," I said. He finally spoke, haltingly:

> I don't want to go to school because it is too early. I don't like the teachers because most of them are too mean. I would like a teacher that is not mean. They fuss at you all the time, they tell you to sit in the back row. They call administrators on you, give you detentions.

I was the one left staring blankly at the computer screen, at a loss for words after he'd finished speaking. It struck me that this was the way this young man *really* felt about school. Janet and I had discussed many times the kind of courage it must take to make a daily return to a place that means constant failure. J.C. had described that failure for me; I hoped this would be a beginning for us.

Explaining to him that we had to have a starting place for change, I asked him how he could make school better. He mumbled something about being more quiet. I then asked him how I could make school better for him. He said that he felt kids should have time to talk, that teachers do all of the talking and never let the kids talk. I agreed, and then asked what we could do in our class to allow students time to talk. He suggested free time. What day? Friday. For how long? Fifteen minutes. I told him that this sounded very reasonable to me. I then asked if all students should have this time. He told me it should be limited to only those that had all of their work done. "Do you feel comfortable bringing this to the rest of the students at the end of class today so that we could have a vote?" I asked. He did.

The class, of course, agreed. They seemed thrilled, and so was someone else for the first time: J.C. I wouldn't exactly say that the expression on his face was one of joy, but there was a slight curve at the corners of his mouth. Finally, I had found a way for him to have a voice in the classroom that wasn't one of anger and hostility.

I had had a breakthrough with J.C.'s writing. I was beside myself and called Janet as soon as I got home that evening. She was happy to finally hear some good news and suggested that feeling comfortable enough to talk with me was the first step. She had worried that his behavior was similar to Kohl's (1991) students who turn "willed refusal to learn into failure to learn." We both hoped that J.C.'s "tantrum" breakthrough meant that he was finally ready to get close to a book.

The following day was independent reading. Again, I invited J.C. to read, showing him the new book that I had bought and read on tape, *The Lion King*. I told him about the other students in the class who had read the book and how much they had seemed to enjoy it. He sat back in the comfortable, orange reading chair, physically distancing himself from the book that I was holding. Please, please, I prayed. "Should I get you a tape player?" I offered. His head nodded just slightly, and he took the book from my outstretched hand. He read the book with the tape that day and for countless other days of independent reading. He then moved to a short biography of Jesse Owens and actually wrote a dialogue journal (Atwell 1987) about it. I sat with him at the computer and typed as he spoke:

Dear Ms. Conry,

The book that I read was *Jesse Owens*. The part that I liked best about this book is when he ran the fifty yard dash in ten seconds. His long jump record was not broken for 25 years. He did the long jump in 26'. I am impressed with the end, when he ran the fifty yard dash in 9.4 seconds.

The part I hated about the book is every winter Jesse Owens caught the flu and one winter he caught the flu and every time he coughed he would cough up blood.

My best character was Jesse Owens. Also, the long jump used to be called the broad jump.

Sincerely,
J.C.

Developing a Reading Habit

After a while, J.C. actually began to find books on his own during independent reading. He loved *Aladdin,* and *Where's Waldo?* seemed to be the choice when he was struggling to find a book that he was comfortable reading. J.C. was only one of many of my students for whom picture books had become a transition into reading. When I mentioned this to Janet, she reminded me of Bishop and Hickman's (1992) words:

The educational values of picture books, however, go beyond their content. Hearing and reading picture books, thinking about and working with them, can help children become better readers and writers. Picture books can also furnish strong support for older readers as they continue in their literacy development. (6)

In Janet's classroom she had surrounded her reluctant readers with picture books because she believed that students couldn't move forward until they had spent time in that lap-reading stage. I was certainly finding the same to be true in our classroom.

Providing Support for Growth

I was thrilled to see J.C. choose to be a part of literacy in our classroom. His behavior in another class, however, landed him back again in I.S.S. I brought him *The Slave Dancer* (Fox 1973), along with a Walkman and the accompanying book on tape. I was a bit apprehensive because this was a longer text and it had no illustrations (a requirement of most of my students for their initial stages of independent reading), but I wanted him to try and branch off into something a bit more challenging. Although J.C.'s face expressed his doubt, I felt confident that he would enjoy and be successful with this adolescent novel. He had participated in shared reading and class discussions regarding strategies for understanding print concepts in longer texts—italics, spacing, and punctuation. We had discussed making predictions and checking our understanding. Like all of the other students, J.C. also had found success in using chapter mapping to aid his comprehension.

I booktalked the novel with him (Bodart 1980), emphasizing the adventure and excitement of the book and downplaying its length, print size, and lack of illustrations. I left him with the book, my fingers crossed. When J.C. appeared in my room during sixth period to say that he needed the second tape, I was elated. In spite of the in-school suspension teacher's complaints that the only work J.C. did was mine, I knew victory when I saw it!

Maintaining Success

J.C.'s success with *The Slave Dancer* helped him find the confidence to continue with longer texts. I asked him if he would be interested in reading the long version of *The Lion King*. He was. Yet I wondered if he would be comfortable jumping into independent rather than assisted reading. Sitting at my desk, we previewed the text together, and he agreed to read the first few paragraphs aloud to me. He struggled with some of the difficult vocabulary and decided that he would like me to read the first few chapters on tape. I knew that J.C. was willing to try a longer text because he had found such a love for the story. This was a vivid reminder to me of the dilemma of teaching nonreaders: How can we expect students to read if their lives have been void of the richness of literature—of fairy tales, fables, and stories? J.C. had found a *story* he loved. His involvement with his initial reading of the picture book version of *The Lion King* had given him the confidence to take a risk with a longer text.

My final challenge for J.C. related to assessment and gave him a choice: Would he prefer to write a dialogue journal or have me write some questions for the first chapters? He decided on the questions. As I watched him curled up in the corner, totally engrossed in his reading, I made myself stop and compare this person to the one who had entered our classroom three weeks into the year. His mood swings, apathy, and rages seemed a thing of the past, but I wanted to keep a picture of that J.C. in my head to remind me that learners can change.

He finished the tape and answered the questions, surprising me with his answers (see Figure 1). I expected him to ask me to read a few more

I am so happy with the work that you completed yesterday. Here are your chapter maps that you wanted to finish. I have also given you some more questions for chapters four, five, and six. See how far you can get, okay?

30/30   30/30

1. Who is the leader of the hyenas? Scar

2. Describe the leader of the hyenas to me. He was smart but could not figh;

3. Tell me a picture that was formed in your head from chapter four. On capter 7 they got stuck by some a masson of thornbushes

4. In chapter five on page 27, what does Simba's father mean when he says, " 'I am only brave when I have to be?'" He don't go looking for trooble

5. What is Scar's plan? to kill simba and mufasa

6. What do you think of this plan? it is going to work

Figure 1.

7. In chapter six on page 29, what does the word "gorge" mean?

It is like A Vally

8. On page 30, what do the three stars, ' ' ', in the middle of the page mean?

Stop a tolk about it change of subject

9. In chapter six, please tell me one picture that was formed in your head.

When He told simba that hi's dad had a sapisive Por him

10. Near the end of chapter six, what does Scar get Simba to believe about his father's death?

that Was the cause of morfasas death

11. Look at your answer to number 10. Why does Scar do this to Simba?

Because hE Want to Ruh away and Never come back then he told the Hycnas to kill simba

12. At the end of chapter six, why does Rafiki run his hand over the picture of young Simba?

because he tought simba was ded'

Figure 1 *cont.*

chapters on tape, but he declined my offer. Once again, I was elated! We discussed how he would process the rest of the text, agreeing that he would draw chapter maps as he felt necessary for the remainder of the book. His artwork was so beautiful that we submitted it to our school literary magazine and he was published (see Figure 2). J.C. had finally made one of the most important reading-writing connections—reading and writing add quality to our lives!

Finding Independence

We ended the school year with a goals project, the result of a discussion I had with Janet regarding the *need* for my students to have a focus for their

Figure 2. *J.C.'s artwork is accepted in the school's literary magazine.*

individual literacy achievements. The students and I discussed the importance of setting goals, what steps needed to be taken to achieve them, and where these goals could take them. We read Michael Jordan's *I Can't Accept Not Trying* (1994), and then each of us set two academic and two personal goals. For the next several weeks, we set aside time on Fridays to write written reflections on the steps that we had taken toward the culmination of our goals. J.C.'s goals were full of voice and honesty (see Figure 3).

He culminated his achievements through his "final exam," where he wrote a list of all the books that he had read during the year in both shared and independent reading. J.C.'s list included the following books:

101 Bossy Cow Jokes   *Jurassic Park* (the short version)
Find Waldo Now   *Where's Waldo?*
The Great Waldo Search   *Beauty and the Beast*
Aladdin   *The Lottery Rose*
The Outsiders   *The Slave Dancer*
Scorpions

J.C. also added a note that "the best two is *The Lion King* and *Jesse Owens.*"

Endings . . .

Janet and I once again discussed J.C.'s progress. We were both thrilled with his response to non-assisted reading and the independence this signaled. She suggested that I have my students write a letter to themselves about what they had accomplished during our time together this year and what they hoped to accomplish next year. When we saw the letter J.C.

> #1   My academic goals are to read more .
> I have done this by independent reading shard reading and reading at home.
> #2 don't talk much so I can hear the teacher #1 don't sit by friend #2 sit in font of class #3 don't chew gum like a cow.
> #1 one of my personal goals is to act better #1 not sitting by my friends.
> #2 not talking back to the teacher #3 do what the teacher says.
> #2 read more better #1 Go some place quiet #2 concentrate on the book you are reading:

Figure 3.

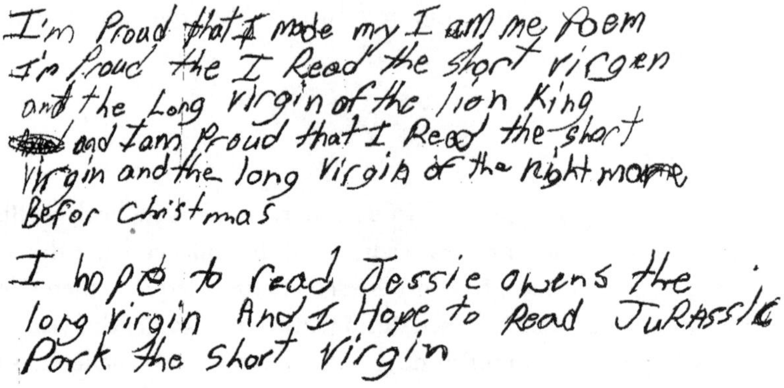

I'm Proud that I made my I am me Poem
i'n Proud the I Read the short viregen
and the Long virgin of the lion King
and I am Proud that I Read the short
Virgin and the long Virgin of the night mare,
Befor Christmas

I hope to read Jessie owens the
long virgin And I Hope to Read JuRASSIc
Pork the short virgin

Figure 4.

wrote (Figure 4), I think we both felt that he finally believed he was capable of literacy—that he was indeed a reader and a writer.

Reflections

I sat at my desk at the end of that last day of school. Our end-of-the-year gathering had left the room littered with paper cups, empty potato chip bags, and candy wrappers. The solitude invited reflection, so I once again picked up J.C.'s letter ". . . the short virgen and the Long virgin. . . ." J.C. really had listened as I offered him longer versions of texts with which he had been successful! As I tried to imagine the wonderful things J.C. could accomplish now that he saw himself as a capable reader and writer, I was reminded of Ralph Fletcher's (1991) words: "There's maybe only one minute in your whole life when you ever do something really important, something that really matters." I knew that in spite of the fact that J.C. was being transferred out of the Literacy Project and into the Emotionally Handicapped Program, our "minute" together had mattered—to all of us.

Bibliography

Atwell, N. 1987. *In the Middle.* Portsmouth, NH: Boynton Cook/Heinemann.

1992. In *Beyond Words: Picture Books for Older Readers,* eds. S. Benedict and L. Carlisle. Portsmouth, NH: Heinemann.

Bettelheim, B., and Zelan, K. 1982. *On Learning to Read: The Child's Fascination with Meaning.* New York: Random House.

Bodart, Joni. 1980. *Booktalk! Booktalking and School Visiting for Young Adult Audiences.* New York: H. W. Wilson.

Fletcher, R. 1991. *Walking Trees.* Portsmouth, NH: Heinemann.

Fox, 1973. *The Slave Dancer.* New York: Dell.

Jordan, M. 1994. *I Can't Accept Not Trying.* New York: HarperCollins.

Kirby, D., and Liner, T. 1988. *Inside Out: Developing Strategies for Teaching Writing.* Portsmouth, NH: Heinemann.

Kohl, H. 1991. *I Won't Learn from You: The Role of Assent in Education.* Minneapolis, MN: Milkweed Editions Publishing.

Myers, Walter Dean. 1990. *Scorpions.* New York: HarperCollins.

Smith, F. 1988. *Joining the Literacy Club.* Portsmouth, NH: Heinemann.

The Voices That Journals Reveal

Judith A. Gosbee

The first day of school. David, a lanky junior, slouches near my desk after class, waiting for my attention. In one glance I notice his black Bulls cap, Metallica shirt, blemished face, and sloping shoulders. "I don't belong in this class," he tells me. "I'm not like these kids." I search his face and sense he's right. The other twenty-eight students look far more confident. David's face reads defeat. I say, "Let's give it a few days. You may be surprised."

Based only on the evidence of David's classroom demeanor, I could have agreed to move him to a less challenging class. But his journal the very first week reveals a wry, self-deprecating wit, a perception of irony beyond his seventeen years, and a greater understanding of literature than most of his classmates have. Each week as I sit to read the journal entries, I pull his out as an early treat. In one he speculates that his "scarlet letter" is a *B* for early baldness, the reason for his cap. In another he writes a hilarious multipage parody of *Ethan Frome*, using his own city as the setting. But anxious not to stand out, he refuses my offer to type it to share with the class. Few know the boy behind the sulky slouch; he makes sure they won't want to.

Like David, most of my students share far more about themselves in their journals than they ever can in class, despite their stylish clothes and hairdos, bright appearances, and "normal" families. For some, the journal becomes a safe haven to experiment and embrace the many selves of adolescence. Elizabeth tries to capture a more playful side by illustrating her notebook with delightful drawings, childlike in their simplicity, whimsical colored pencil prewriting hints. I suspect she draws these before writing, making the words fit all around the image, perhaps providing the focus she needs to begin. I learn of Elizabeth's first ski experience, questions about God, closeness to her sister, Girl Scout responsibilities, dancing lessons, and loyalties. The Elizabeth I see in class only speaks when called on, assuming that others' opinions matter first. She hides her playful self with dull clothes and a plain face. Though it is impossible to sound the depth of her character by her class contributions, I know her well by what she tells me in her writing.

I know her so well I want to pair her with another junior named Gary, a serious political science buff who writes long, rhyming poems about presidents and war. He needs whimsy but doesn't trust it, keeping his eyes down, only letting a smile escape when he just can't help it. Nevertheless, he understands the weaknesses and contradictions in human nature. As formal in his journal as with himself, distrustful of emotions, wary of the "nerd" jeers he is sure are one word away, Gary breaks rank and explores feelings of grief and love when his uncle dies. Later, overcome by the kindness of a classmate he had not expected to like, Gary writes of his discovery in a conversational tone he's never used out loud. By June some of his smiles are saved for laughing with himself about his seriousness.

Journals help me to read what is behind the faces I see in my classes. I am constantly amazed by the hidden sides students never share aloud. But it is easy to see why they can't, even in a safe classroom. Rejection is too big a risk. I remember well the loneliness of that rejection and isolation.

In 1963, my parents separated and I moved from a small town to a city in another state. My father and I shared a furnished apartment. I began eleventh grade in a large high school where I had no friends. I sat in the library, watching groups all around me sharing stories of weekend fun. No one asked me who I was. That year I feigned illness sixty-eight times, writing notes in my father's hand. No one asked where I was—not the nurse, not my teachers, not the principal, and especially not the guidance counselor.

The isolation I felt more than thirty years ago is experienced by many adolescents today. Theirs is a loneliness born of feeling that no one else experiences their pain; everyone is happy except them. Even in classrooms where students collaborate in groups, individuals seldom reveal much of a personal nature. The risks of "being different" are far too great. Yet, invited to write every day in a journal, they welcome the chance to talk about the real issues of their lives. For many, it is the only invitation they have ever had to write about what matters to them.

Journals are an invitation into my class, into a shared experience of discovery. They provide a window for me to see lives too often ignored not only by schools but also by families. In the past eight years that I have used journals as a regular part of my class, I've seen an alarming increase in the number of students who say their parents are either too busy, too damaged, or too alienated to offer adult influence in their lives. Despite the value kids place on peer opinion, they want an adult sounding-board to test the validity of their ideas. Most are experimenting with notions of who they are by embracing an idea one day and rejecting it the next. The journal page becomes a place to entertain ideas without having to commit to them entirely. It's the dance between the notion and the action: the place to find out what to keep and what to discard. Adolescence is a time of great flux. Unfortunately, most students simply live it. The journal allows them the additional luxury of reflection.

During the course of the year, I ask students to write five full pages per week in their journals. On a designated day each week, I flip through the pages to briefly note the length and content of the entries as I stamp each page. Then students select a page to turn in. When I first assigned journals, I read all five pages. Besides being very time-consuming, it inhibited some students from writing about sensitive issues important for them to explore. Students know that the subject of any entry they do not turn in is private. Allowing them to choose the entry they want me to read often means the content is more significant than entries about mall trips and football practice, though I still get a share of those. Whether the writers choose to explore weighty issues or not, ultimately, all the writing is instructive because students are practicing putting their thoughts on paper without the pressure of a grade.

At the end of the year I ask students to re-read all their entries and note the patterns they find there. They look at content, style, length, genre, risk, and degree of investment in their writing. For some in my class, this is the first time they have looked closely at their own words. In doing so, they make very important discoveries.

Last year, Stacey, whose journals always made me laugh, said,

Many times I found myself writing out of confusion . . . about things I didn't understand. I found in later journal entries that through time I had answered my own questions. Then I became confused as to how I did that! And TA-DAH! A journal was born!

In the same evaluation conference, she added,

> After I read my journals, I felt like I was reading about someone else. I'm not a self-proclaimed Sybil, it's just that I was surprised to see how I had changed over a nine-month course. My friends, ideas, goals, and attitude had had their ups and downs, but in the end came out pretty good.

Her words echo the words of many others who marvel at the changes they see in themselves. If we don't ask them to notice, they don't learn that "in the end" the problems can get resolved, even if it's just to a point of being "pretty good." For Stacey, who was taking both junior and senior English courses after nearly quitting school, this was a very significant discovery. Too many kids never recognize that life may, and probably will, get better over time.

Reflecting on their own words helps students to take responsibility for a greater part of their lives because they see themselves as vehicles for change. In fact, many have said that the journal became a way to maintain self-control. Stacey noted,

> Rather than saying something to someone that I would later regret, I wrote it down. I was able to vent a lot of my anger and frustrations out on paper and receive credit for it at the same time!

Another student said:

> Writing helped me understand my feelings more and it let out all of the trapped emotions I had locked up inside me.

Having a place to examine their feelings, memories, thoughts, and experiences offers a wealth of benefits for adolescents, especially those who do not have an adult outlet for discussion. I'm reminded that even in families with two parents who care deeply for their children, silences, secrets, and miscommunications are common. Teenagers need a safe place to air ideas —even the ones they will subsequently reject.

The necessity for a private place to record their thoughts makes it essential that I read only what students wish to share. Having that choice allows them the freedom to take risks they might not otherwise venture. It also underscores the importance of entries that are shared: these are what matter. As part of the initial assignment I explain that I am not a guidance counselor; therefore, if they choose to write about danger to themselves or others, I must inform those who are equipped to help. Three years ago I received four journal entries from girls from three different classes all about a mutual friend who was being physically abused by her boyfriend. These four students saw their journals as a vehicle for getting help for a friend they cared about. (They had planned what they would say to ensure that I would notice.) In the course of the year, many students seek help not only for their friends but for themselves through their shared pages. If journals serve no other end than to enable students to get help in crisis situations, they are well worth doing.

Most of the pages I receive speak of the whole spectrum of experiences from taking a special family trip to losing a loved one. In many, students write to let me know who they are. Sometimes they begin slowly, sharing sports victories or memories of school trips. As the weeks roll by, they learn to trust me with more significant pieces of themselves: births, deaths, joys, fears, beginnings, endings, attitudes, reactions, hates, and loves. I respond with short notes, often asking questions; sometimes what they write spurs me to write more. I ask for honest words, and they expect the same. Our conversations on paper become the unspoken adhesive of the class. They connect teens to a place where they know they belong.

Most students today—even those without physical and mental disabilities or difficult home lives—face obstacles to being successful in school. If I can give them a way to connect their lives to school, if I can enable them to communicate their concerns, if I can invite them into the school community by saying, "I need your voice here," then I offer more than simple coping skills. For many, it is a chance to find the voice they have never been asked to use.

Tom, a chain-smoking snowboarder, observed:

These journal assignments have been very beneficial to me for the simple reason that they have taught me to introduce my ideas in my writing. When I'm just sitting around and I get an idea, I write it down now so I can include it into my writing assignments. You may not believe this, but I swear to god on my life it is true. I find by doing this it saves me a lot of time . . .

Even without the oath, I believe Tom because others also voice surprise that they can be the kind of students who actually sit down and record ideas to use later. Too often students feel they must use a "school" voice in their writing, a voice they can never hope to find. Tom sees that his words have validity. He is also seeing that he has found a way to improve in the class. This may be Tom's first revelation about what successful students do and his first realization that he, too, can succeed.

Finding their own voices, especially for previous nonwriters, boosts students' confidence that they have something to say. Ultimately, this leads to greater fluency. Danny said:

> I think these journals have helped me to progress in my writing skills. . . . For example, in the beginning of the year, oftentimes I would have difficulty completing a single page. By the end of the year, I could complete a page with relative ease. By the end of the year, I found out there was a writer inside me. I had written in the past, but never in such high volume as this year.

Certainly Danny might have discovered his love of writing some other way through more structured class writing assignments, but for him, the joy was in the self-discovery of exploring his own topics; playing with words and forms; venturing into a dialogue about himself; risking showing it to someone else; and finding not only that is it fun, but also that he is good at it! Note that Danny didn't need me to tell him he had a writer inside, but he did need someone to invite him to make that discovery himself. His definition of a "good writer" and ours may differ, yet his interest in writing makes him receptive to knowing how to get better. He has a vested interest in becoming better because *he* has discovered the writer within himself.

As an English teacher, I want my students to write well. Yet I recognize that getting them to do so requires more than lessons on form and content. Good writers know they have something to say; therefore, they want to say it effectively. For me and my students, journals become, as one football player put it, "the playing field" for ideas. After years of reading too many content-insipid yet form-correct essays, I know that journals give students ideas for meaningful topics, ones worth shaping into something more. In addition, journals help me become more aware of what aspects of their writing need fine-tuning. Many of my lessons come directly from what I observe in the journals. Also, because I am familiar with their interests, I can even prompt the reluctant writers with an idea I've already heard them express. Therefore, the journals become a teaching tool as well.

Beyond its use educationally and socially, journal writing has helped me to focus on students. After all, they are the reason I teach. In many ways, I think I am the main beneficiary of their journal pages. Years after they've graduated and I've forgotten their names, I can recall the football player's entry about rocking his baby sister to sleep or the ice skater's frustration with trying a new jump. I can see the faces of all the silent ones who wrote about the important matters of their lives.

I wonder whether Dave learned to play the guitar and if he found someone else who loved to read his writing. Is Elizabeth still drawing pictures? Did Gary ever find a girl like Elizabeth to help him find his playful side, or is he still writing political poems? Maybe one of them will write me a letter someday and let me know. For now, I am content that during the year I was with them, their voices were heard.

Kien
Learning to Write in a Second Language

Judy Bebelaar

K*ien wore her* long, black hair like a veil. All she had to do was bend forward across her desk slightly, and it fell, hiding her from the teacher and the class. Her written English was difficult to understand sometimes, because of grammar and vocabulary problems; her voice, on the rare occasions she spoke, was soft. She was excruciatingly shy. But she completed every assignment, thoroughly and conscientiously.

By the time I met Kien, I was lucky; I had a classroom of my own, no longer moving from floor to floor as I had for the first two years. My new "home" was in the school basement and was originally an old office or storeroom. It was small. The school itself, a lovely Spanish-style building built in 1921, was run-down and overcrowded. The school dumpster sat outside my windows, which were boarded up because there had been many break-ins by homeless people. Mice, bad smells, and roaches were a problem, but it was *my* room. One of my students made a beautiful graffiti wall with "Creative Writing" written above the images. It's still there, after all these years.

Good Intentions

Kien entered my sophomore English class at a time when I was still using Warriner's grammar book, explaining lessons and assigning homework. I had many students like Kien, who was Cambodian, and others who grew up speaking Chinese or Spanish or Tagalog—students recently out of English-as-a-Second-Language classes whom I believed still needed to learn more about the structure of the language they were acquiring. While I knew that research said the textbook approach to grammar didn't help, I felt real ambivalence about what was the best way to help students like Kien and her American-born inner-city classmates. So out of the best intentions, I set aside part of two days a week to correct the Warriner's grammar homework aloud in class, discussing the reasons for this being proper standard English and that not, taking home piles of grammar quizzes to correct, and giving tests on participial phrases, gerunds, and predicate nominatives.

I tried to correct every grammatical error on an essay and, if I had time, write an explanation of the rule. However, my students looked utterably bored during grammar. Often, too many people had all the correct answers on their homework but obviously didn't understand the reasons at all. Worse yet, when I made part of the final a grammar test, the scantron electronic marking machine clicked away remorselessly, letting me and everyone else in the faculty workroom know that my students were getting many more wrong answers than right ones. In spite of all that, I kept trying. I blamed myself for not making the grammar lessons interesting enough. I tried to think of grammar games. I explained creatively. I gave examples I hoped were funny enough to make students laugh and remember: "Wondering what to do next, the clock struck twelve. Of *course,* the *clock* wasn't wondering what to do next!" My audience remained silent.

A New Way

It was not until the following year, when Kien signed up for my Creative Writing class, that I was able to find a truly effective way to improve students' grammar. In that class, I did not directly teach grammar except to help students prepare work for publication. Katharine Harer, who had a California Arts Council grant to work as a poet-in-residence at the school, team-taught with me twice a week. Other poets visited the class, too. Katharine and I presented model poems and prose pieces by our favorite writers to stimulate student writing. We gave students permission to follow the writer's phrasing and sentence structure as closely as they liked. This hands-on experience became a catalyst to improving students' grammar.

Kien's growth as a writer and her increasing sophistication in the use of English is reflected in examples of her work as a junior and senior in my Creative Writing class:

Mess

My life is a mess
My room is a mess
My binder is a mess
My hair is a mess
My friends are a mess
My teachers are a mess
My school is a mess
Love is a mess
This world is a mess
That's why my life is a mess

Grandmother

Sometimes I find my grandmother in my room
just sitting there in the dark peeling
an orange
But her mind isn't on the orange
Her mind is somewhere else
I know what she's thinking
I don't have to look at her to know that
she is sad
I know sometimes she cries
It makes my heart ache
The death of her brother
Cher Wang

Kien's later poems are longer and use much more sophisticated sentence structure. In the following poem, she frees herself from the models we were presenting, Genny Lim's "Yellow Woman," Carl Sandburg's "Chicago," and Jane Cortez's "I Am New York City":

Cambodia

I was the palm trees that swayed to the morning breeze
I was the blue water that flowed down the cascade

I was the laughter that echoed in everyone's heart
I was the magnificent Ankor Wat that received many prayers
I was the little girl going to school with my friends down that crooked
    road
I was tomorrow that brought a new day

I was Cambodia

I am Pol Pot,
The leader of the Khmer Rouge
who knows only the meaning of death
I am the hideous bombs that kill thousands of innocents
I am the heart that beats like a drum every night
I am the bodies that rot in that muddy road
I am the ground that carries a burden of deaths on
my shoulders
I am the sky that deceives the eyes
I am the planes that had death written all over them
I am the bodies that rot in that muddy road
I am the deceitful sky that lies to the naive
infants
Being thrown up high like
Targets into that deadly sword

I am Cambodia

This poem, as well as several others at this level of sophistication, was published in our anthology that year, *We Are Twilight When Bright Lights Start to Fall*. Kien's successful shift from the past to the present tense is part of what makes the poem work. The shift from the first stanza to the second shows not only her ability to use tenses correctly (a real problem for ESL students), but also her skill at using past and present tense for emotional effect.

The writers, Katharine, or I read their poems aloud almost every day. After the students' confidence in their abilities as writers developed, their own work became the models. Following models gives students whose first language is not English a chance to do what American-born students do—pick up grammar and phrasing by ear. Then they play with the language, so grammar and sentence structure come naturally, without all the tedious and ineffective explication of a formal grammar lesson. More important, the syntax and phrasing the students are emulating is the best—the most beautiful and varied.

Kien continued to write reams. She completed the class assignments and then went home and wrote more. She had a great deal she wanted to say—about Cambodia, about her observations of this country, about her inner life. As she wrote, her grasp of the language became more complex, as the following two-line haiku illustrates:

The wind washed my face
But it didn't wash away my blues.

Her grammar improved. The sentences flowed more naturally. She still made some errors, but the syntax wasn't as tangled. While I knew that, according to research, teaching grammar out of context has minimal effect on improving writing, Kien taught me to be sure of the reason. Very few people have a burning desire to be correct for the sake of correctness. It's the desire to express what's in your heart—so aptly, so movingly that others can readily and truly connect—which motivates you to write and rewrite. It's when you are thoroughly engaged in the writing process that the phrasing from a piece of writing that hooked you floats to the surface of your mind. That's when the light goes on and something tells you, "Yes, that's it."

You and I Are the Same

You and I are the same
but we don't let our hearts see

Black, White and Asian
Africa, China, United States and all other
countries around the world

Peel off their skin
like you peel an orange

See their flesh
like you see my heart

Peel off their meat
and peel my wickedness with it too
until there's nothing left
but bones

Then you will see that you and I
are the same

She became a truly gifted writer, and won an honorable mention for her
poetry at a humanities festival in which most of the participants were students at private schools in the Bay Area. That day, Kien read strongly and
beautifully in front of the other students and the three judges, who were
professional poets. One of the judges pulled her aside later in the day to
tell her she had real talent. Here are two of the poems she read:

Red Sky

at 6:45 PM
after the rain
a patch of reddish-pink sky forms
like a crimson rose petal
behind those bare empty gray boughs
it seems as if the evening sun
rises from that tree
against the sunset sky

my yard glows
as if god were in that patch
of red sky

The 30 Bus

The 30 bus was full
Full of mostly dark haired
People with the sun's coat
Two Chinese old women were sitting in the front
Talking greedily
Loud and sharp
Like two hens stealing the
Morning worms from the Earth
Cantonese was flowing from students' tongues

And the bodies were stacked and pulled
As tight as a rope

A tall white man

With blond hair and blue eyes
In his three piece suit
With his black leather brief case
Stung them with words that
Scarred my heart
"Don't you people have cars?" he said loud and clear
in his white sarcastic tongue
The talking stopped
The people stared at each other
Stunned
My heart sank into a
Deep blue icy sea

Kien had mastered the language well enough to compete with students who not only were native born, but also were very skilled in using English. Later that year, she became the only high school student to win a prize in the *San Francisco Bay Guardian*'s annual poetry contest, a very popular competition. Her own efforts to produce, to polish, and to publish her work account for most of her dramatic development, certainly not my early efforts to teach her grammar out of a Warriner's book.

Kien Finds Her Voice

Kien's writer's voice was heard, literally, when she participated in another Creative Writing class project. The students had written a play, *Broken Arrow,* based on the idea of qualities represented by human characters. The play was inspired by Ruth Gendler's *The Book of Qualities* and fleshed out with inspiration from Katharine, help from a student teacher whose real love was drama, and guidance from a local actor-director. Kien portrayed "Loneliness," sitting at her desk with her hair over her face. In the first version of the play, she had one brief line to speak to "Depression": "I just want to be left alone, OK?" We worked hard on her being *loud* enough and *angry* enough.

When we decided to produce the play again, as Katharine got permission for us to use a beautiful little theater that was better designed acoustically than the cavernous school auditorium, Kien came in with yet another extra assignment. She'd written "Loneliness" a longer speech. She approached "Depression" again, to tell her, "I'm sorry I yelled at you. It's just that it hurts when people use me. When nobody's around, they talk to me, but when their friends are there, it's like I'm invisible." Kien delivered her lines with passion, even more loudly than some of the others. The rest of the cast applauded Kien, knowing just how much she had grown.

I believe Kien's impressive progress as a writer and speaker of a new language was sparked by several aspects of the Creative Writing class. First, writing from models helped produce writing with more elegant and complex syntax. This technique provided Kien with examples to work with, an experience she would have missed if she had been limited to writing from "scratch." The fact that we shared student writing was important as well. Students weren't merely responding to great writers, they were developing their own voices. Along the way, their work was honored by publication. By spring, Kien no longer required a chorus of the entire class to convince her to lift that dark veil of hair and read one of her poems.

We always produced an anthology of student poetry and a multicultural calendar containing student work. Poems went to the school paper, to poetry contests, and to the "Poem of the Month" contest Katharine and I sponsored, in which one poem was chosen by a team of students to put on a colorful flyer and post in the school hallways, the library, and the gym.

Probably the most important factor in Kien's growth was the influence of the class itself. We worked hard at creating a community of writers. Working together to produce the anthology, calendar, and play and sharing poems which were often personal helped us form a close-knit group.

Kien in College

Kien is now at the University of California at Davis and wrote me about how she took part in demonstrations there to protest school budget cuts and hikes in student fees. She's getting good grades, and she's taking a poetry class. Sometimes, she sends me her writing:

Ancient Trees

Close your eyes
Put yourself under a
Giant Sequoia
Sit in a lotus position

Do not stir
Clear your mind and
Concentrate on your breath
Now imagine yourself

Walking through an Ancient Forest in
Western Oregon
Look to your right
See the 250 foot Douglas fir
With 800 years to its name
Look up at it from its massive trunk
Up and up until you think your neck is
Going to break
If you bend it any further

There you will see
A spot of blueness that manages to
Pierce its head through the leaves and branches
See a streak of white light like Zeus's
Thunderbolt
Coming from it
Revealing the mystic
Dust motes
That the shadows hide

Remember
Do not open your eyes
And
Do not stir
Just take a deep breath
Now imagine
Men Bulldozers Vast Chains Saws
Destroying the massive Calm of Nature

Hear the cries of the Spotted Owls
See the Douglas fir
With chains tied around its gigantic trunk
Being uprooted from the hand of the
Earth that holds its soul

See 800 years of breath
Vanish like the last star of the night

Conclusion

When Kien was still in my class, some of the students went to a local radio station to advertise the calendar. The host of the show asked one student, Kim, "Isn't it hard, all of you from such different backgrounds, learning to get along well enough to do a project like the calendar?"

"No," Kim replied, "because when we share what we've written, we learn that we've all had pretty hard roads to travel."

That is what Kien had a chance to share: the hard road. There is something transformative about recreating and then transmuting a difficult time into a record or a tribute or a paean. Writing moves one from recording the painful to bearing witness, from recounting experience to creating art—and, often, learning the complexities and beauty of a new language along the way.

Kien has found her voice and it's beautiful.

Bibliography

Cortez, Jane. 1989. "I Am New York City," *Coagulations: New and Selected Poems.* New York: Thunder's Mouth Press.

Gendler, J. Ruth. 1988. *The Book of Qualities.* New York: Harper and Row.

Lim, Genny. 1989. *Winter Place.* San Francisco: Kearny Street Press.

Po, Kien. 1994. "Ancient Trees." Unpublished.

———. 1990. "Cambodia," *We Are Twilight When Bright Lights Start to Fall.* San Francisco: Galileo Creative Writing Club.

———. 1989. "Grandmother," *Time Is Winding Up.* San Francisco: Galileo Creative Writing Club.

———. 1989. "Haiku," San Francisco: Galileo Creative Writing Club.

———. 1989. "Mess," San Francisco: Galileo Creative Writing Club.

———. 1990. "Red Sky," *We Are Twilight When Bright Lights Start to Fall.* San Francisco: Galileo Creative Writing Club.

———. 1990. "The 30 Bus," San Francisco: Galileo Creative Writing Club.

————. 1989. "You and I Are the Same," *Time Is Winding Up*. San Francisco: Galileo Creative Writing Club.

Sandburg, Carl. 1988. "Chicago," *American Poetry*, ed. Charles Sullivan. New York: Harry N. Abrams.

Warriner, John E. 1988. *English Composition and Grammar*. Orlando, FL: Harcourt Brace Jovanovich.

Anonymous Team Journals
New Identity, New Voice

Bruce Greene

In recent years a shadowy figure has entered my classroom. It is an amorphous entity that finds particular comfort in class discussions. Composed of equal parts of fear, arrogance, and apathy, this thief is as loud as a disparaging remark heard by all, or as silent as the astonishing stillness that can accompany a profound question allowed to die in public.

Most teachers can identify with the following scene. You've read a particularly inspiring short story or viewed a poignant film or watched a shocking piece of news footage. The class has focused on a passage that raises a vital issue, something they need to discuss NOW! They are all there with you in that moment. Nothing else matters. You can see it in their faces; you can see it in their eyes. You can almost see the wheels turning. Recognizing the importance of the moment, you keep it going just a bit longer. Suddenly, from the far reaches of your classroom, there comes a hand. It is attached to an arm that is attached to a body that seldom participates in these moments. You are delighted. The eyes are electric, the face is almost smiling. You call on the student, and just before this student speaks, there comes that sound. Sometimes it is a "tsk," sometimes it is a whispered phrase accompanied by a look shot with military precision. From the once eager participant comes only "Never mind," or "Nothing, I forgot what I wanted to say." Maybe the response is silent, just a meek nod that proclaims, "I'm out, forget it."

Throughout my years in the classroom, I've noticed that class discussions are very fragile organisms. They grow, expand, bloom, and die, sometimes within seconds, but always right before my eyes. As a beginning social science teacher, I cut my teeth on the Socratic method. I recall setting goals for discussions—goals that included involving as many students as possible. When students start generating their own questions and start asking each other those questions, that is nirvana. Yet as class discussions progressively became less than satisfying, it was my own questions that multiplied. Given that most kids love to talk and have a good deal to say, why had some classes become so quiet? What was going on inside the heads of students who didn't or wouldn't participate? In what I'd thought of as good class discussions, what really went on during this seemingly stimulating exchange of ideas? Who talked? Who didn't? I wondered, too, how I should judge the quality of class discussion in my classroom. These questions would not leave me alone.

Lauren Muller, a fellow Bay Area Writing Project teacher-consultant, had faced similar questions in teaching a Native American Literature class at the University of California at Berkeley. She noticed that often the Native American students in her classes had the least to say. "They were often the most knowledgeable, the ones who had the most to contribute to discussions," she said. To address this dilemma, Muller introduced anonymous team journals. Two years ago, I introduced anonymous team journals in my own classroom.

For the past ten years, I have taught both English and social science. My classes, like siblings, differ widely in behavior and attitude. While some are termed "accelerated," all contain an ethnically diverse, for the most part motivated, student population. Despite high energy levels, even the most dedicated students, the most talented writers, could be uncommonly quiet during discussions. In fact, a haunting discrepancy between what they wrote and what they said seemed to prevail. Their prose often contained all that I hoped would come out during class discussions. What would the addition of the anonymous team journal do to the emotional quality and content of the topics my students discussed? Would some students be more willing "to discuss" in writing? Would they reveal what inhibits them from speaking in class? I wondered, too, if these team journals would affect or even improve the oral discussions in class.

Logistics were going to be a problem. As the school year began, I divided each of my classes of thirty to thirty-five students into six teams. Each student was randomly assigned a number, one through six, and a day of the week, Monday through Friday. In classes of more than thirty students we called the remaining students "floaters." They could pick any number and join that team, so that each team would have at least five members while some had six.

We then chose pseudonyms. I asked that no one choose a name that might be offensive or inappropriate, but they were free to choose any name. The students loved choosing false names. Some women chose men's names, some men chose women's names. Many chose poetic, humorous, or mysterious names. They called themselves *The Great Pretender, Crystal Tiger, Ming Li,* and *Major Woody.* Sometimes their names spoke volumes—names like *Marilyn Manson, Holey Random,* and *1890.* Very little time was wasted in the name-choosing process, which proved to be an immediate hook. I could see, instantly, that these students were not hiding behind a name. Instead, they were creating a new identity. This was not going to be a gimmick. These students were, in fact, liberating themselves. Into the team journals appeared the likes of *Mute, Secret Passion,* and *Quintessence.* Introducing themselves to one another were *Peaches, Pinky, Ocean, Alex, Naive,* and *Best Burrito.*

Writing in the team journals was only one small part of my curriculum. It was done daily, weekly, as an ongoing feature, but in no way did it ever become the dominant activity. We read, wrote, and discussed as always. I-Search papers (Macrorie 1984) and *The Grapes of Wrath* came and went like homecoming and the junior prom. But always, my students were exchanging ideas. They were often critical of one another but with an increased passion. With the new names came new voices.

When I first imagined how the team journals would work, I envisioned students discussing literature or current affairs. I hoped that many of the issues surfacing in our class discussions would find their way into the team journals. I could see endless pondering about a literary character's motivation, an author's style, or a current national dilemma. To be sure, there was some of this. But the team journals took on their own life and became much more than a place where small groups could exchange ideas. They became a mirror, if not a time capsule, of both my students' lives and the school year. What emerged in most of the exchanges, whether they were related to literature or topics under consideration in class, were issues and events going on in these kids' lives now.

A typical literature-based exchange occurred when one class was reading John Steinbeck's *In Dubious Battle. Roxanne* wrote:

What do you guys think about being willing to die . . . and sacrificing your life for the benefit of future generations? Honestly, I give these guys so much credit . . . but I don't think I'd have the balls or the faith to stick it out. I know that sounds horrible but it's human nature to look at the immediate effects, not the big picture. I guess that's why I liked the book so much, these guys saw things from an amazing point of view. At times I thought they were cold-hearted, but I realized they had the warmest hearts of anyone. What do you think?

Bob responded,

I guess I never took notice of the book's significance. But now that I think about it, I'm pretty sure I could not be as enduring or courageous as Mac or Jim, unless the importance of the issue affected me deeply.

Two other team members joined in the discussion, one adding that she was behind in the reading but now had some motivation to catch up. *Secret Passion* added,

The book really isn't as bad as I thought it was, I judged it too quickly, Sorree!

As I had hoped, these private discussions did seem to influence class members. Aside from providing an additional forum for expressing and clarifying ideas about the literature we read, they were actually, in some cases, providing an incentive to complete the readings on time.

I have always been sensitive to the issue of relevance when selecting literature or suggesting specific works for individual students. Before beginning any novel, play, short story, or work of nonfiction with a class, I generally try to find a link to my students' lives. Often their writing assignments reinforce that connection. The team journals began to reflect those relationships in ways I never could have expected. From reading and discussing *The Catcher in the Rye* came the following written exchange:

BOB: Do you guys ever feel like school is just so fake? Like everybody is unreal, not their true selves. . . .
ROXANNE: I do feel like this school's fake! 100%! Remember how I was saying before that I thought I was crazy for relating to Holden Caulfield? Well, that's exactly why! I'm so glad you said that Bob, I feel so much better.

As the school year progressed, these links became a regular feature of team journal discussion—so much so that in-class crises were beginning to be discussed within the journals' pages as well. One such turning point came while an English class was reading Charles Fuller's drama *A Soldier's Play*. While reading, one student had some momentary difficulty with her lines. "Just read!" snapped a frustrated classmate. The faltering reader had been "dissed bigtime." The class looked at me. I stared back and then suggested we continue with a bit more sensitivity to each other. Within days the incident surfaced in the team journals. *1890* wrote:

> I find it ironic that here we are in English reading a play about hatred and how it destroys people, everyone oohs and aahs about how horrible it all is and yet I see people playing the same kind of games in our classroom. When a certain person, who shall remain nameless, would make a mistake in the reading, people were rude and intolerant. Some people laughed, they thought it was funny . . . because she's not like everyone else, that makes it OK. When another person, who "fits in" made the same mistake while reading, nobody said anything; people smiled nice polite smiles. Does it bother you that people only feel their own injustices?

This entry turned into a rather long discussion of how a peer group can rob each other of self-esteem, little by little. *1890* cautioned her classmates not to

> sit there feeling hurt and wronged by someone else's ignorance and get so rolled up in your own pain . . . that [you] sit there and complain and then turn around and do the same damn thing to someone else. Nobody deserves to be treated the way some of us treat that person.

I felt compelled to read that entry to the class. The issues in our lives and the literature we read were beginning to overlap, and together we were finding new ways to deal with them.

So what have I learned, and what can I say about the impact of something called an anonymous team journal? What surfaces for me is exactly what I've come to believe is behind any effective class discussions: trust. This includes a nonjudgmental peer response and the acceptance that part of the learning process is trying on new thoughts and different ideas in public. The team journals allow students who feel "shot down" in class discussions to be heard. They often drop their inhibitions because they realize, some for the first time, that nobody will interrupt them. I've learned that students have what one colleague of mine termed "ancient perceptions of themselves," and that for many, the new identity provided by a new name changes this perception.

Because they demand honesty, the journals, like verbal discussions, create vulnerability. More than once I read comments that criticized my remarks in class or to particular students. More than once I realized that the human community that materializes before my eyes in five versions daily is infinitely more complex than I think. The journals are a risk, a leap of faith at worst, another teacher in the classroom at best, for the students and me. Sometimes that other teacher tells me truths I could learn in no other way. I recall a particularly animated, hostile discussion I had with an International Problems class during the last days of apartheid in South Africa. As the most vocal students were projecting their own anger and insecurities toward one another under the guise of political rhetoric, I played my usual mediator role hoping and helping to promote understanding. Emotions still ran high as the bell rang and the weekend began. Physically drained, I gathered books and papers, closed windows, and prepared to leave it all behind for two days, while a few students completed writing in the journals. The room was now empty, the lights out, the door closing. Suddenly I reached for a team journal. The final entry for the week was a brief, heartfelt piece about how fortunate this particular student felt to be studying South Africa. I left smiling.

Bibliography

Fuller, Charles. 1981. *A Soldier's Play*. New York: Hill and Wang. A division of Straus and Giroux.

Macrorie, Ken. 1984. *Searching Writing*. Upper Montclair, NJ: Boynton/Cook.

Muller, Lauren. 1993. "Collaborative 'Life Stories' and Anonymous Team Journals: Fostering Dialogue and Decentering Authority in the Classroom." *American Quarterly,* Vol. 45, No. 4 (December 1993), 598–611.

Salinger, J. D. 1945. *The Catcher in the Rye*. New York: Little Brown and Company.

Steinbeck, John. 1936. *In Dubious Battle*. New York: Viking Penguin, Inc.
———. 1939. *The Grapes of Wrath*. New York: The Viking Press Inc.

✺ *Lunchroom Conversation*

Mike McCormick

Ish bites his soggy burrito
carefully
so none of the filling
spills
onto his white basketball jacket.

His older brother was shot twelve hours ago
and he's trying to puzzle out the story
from a crumpled newspaper clipping
that he grips in his other hand. It says the police will
question all suspects.

Turning to his friend Willie, talking slow
he announces, "When the cop at the door said he was sorry
Mom fell to the floor screaming. Screaming,
you know, like in church when you feel the gospel
or get touched by the Holy Spirit.

"Mom told him not to go,
told him to stay and watch t.v.
but he said 'I'm leaving'
and went. It's his own fault he got killed,
if he'd listened he wouldn't of got hit.

"Don't get me wrong, I got sorrow
but I ain't got no tears.
They're gonna wait to do the burying
'til the ground thaws. I might cry at the funeral
when I see him laid out in the casket."

As Willie stands to go,
Ish asks, "Do you think my Mom will get some money
because of the killing?"
Willie looks straight in his face and says, "It don't pay to get killed.
The government don't care much about it."

A Community of Learners

Fran Wong

Where Learning Takes Place

Last year, for the first time in my teaching career, I became a floater—no homeroom, just an office to call home base. I had relinquished my seventh-grade English classroom when I accepted some administrative duties, and so, according to my new schedule, I would meet my classes in one of four possible rooms available on a rotating schedule.

Not having a classroom after twenty years of teaching posed a number of challenges. For one, I was an English teacher without a classroom library. After checking around for an unused library bookcart and finding that none were available, I fixed up my own traveling library. I purchased two large plastic boxes and piled in the books. Then I used a luggage cart to wheel the library from class to class. The books were borrowed from both my school library and from our public state library. For each new project, I'd change the library's contents. The students became accustomed to picking up the library at my office and then returning it after a class. They seemed to sense that the books were really for them, and therefore they took the responsibility of making sure it was present during class.

At first I was a bit leery of creating a portable library with materials that I didn't own. But not once were the books lost or abused. I had a deep sense that the students appreciated the chance to browse through them, share them with a friend, and have materials to use beyond what they themselves had brought to class. For this year I have ordered an official bookcart—yet somehow, those two plastic boxes coming down the lanai [corridor] on a luggage cart had real character.

That problem being solved, I next turned to the dilemma of bulletin boards. Where could I display the future work of my young writers? And what about those literary units that required students to build the boards as they acquired new insights? I studied each of the four classrooms. Not one inch of bulletin board space was available. And even if I were to claim a small niche of my own, I was faced with the hard reality that the class didn't meet in the same room every day. My eyes scanned the rooms, the floors, the ceilings, the closet doors, the wooden locker faces. The wooden locker faces were perfect! Each room had wooden lockers or small cupboards for students to store their gear. They were really shelves, which had been partitioned, and each partitioned section was fitted with a door for privacy. You could easily post a 9" × 11" piece of construction paper on each door face. True, I had to cut down the dimensions of the projects a bit, but the students were more than happy to have their work put up. As for projects that required active building throughout a class, I located two portable bulletin boards, one for each English class. Again the students came through to willingly cart the boards to and from class.

Finally, there was the problem of my teaching materials. I no longer had everything available within an arm's reach. I had to carry everything I needed in a stout canvas bag. Before class, I'd go through the ritual of packing my bag: student papers, tests, handouts, texts, books for enriching a lesson, grade book, pens, pencils, special supplies for a particular unit, book orders, keys. Inevitably, I'd forget an item or realize in the middle of a discussion that something stashed away in my office would have been extremely useful! I am an organized person, but it was an eye-opening and humbling experience. I had always expected kids to come prepared for class and not forget to bring their materials. But now, somehow, it didn't matter quite so much. After all, the students were there, I was there, the materials could be shared; the learning could take place.

Trying to Accommodate a Variety of Voices

I would like to have better oral reading and speaking because I'm constantly stuttering.

Tony

My goal is to have better study habits. I chose this because I want better grades on my quizzes and tests.

Nel

One of my goals is to be more cooperative when I work in a group so everyone will get along and that way more things can get done.

Felix

I wish to learn how to make great stories because I want people to get interested in my stories after the first couple of sentences. . . . I also want to learn new words to put in my vocabulary, so when I speak I don't use baby words.

Simone

I want to learn to study better.

Selina

I hope to improve my vocab skills . . . I'm not good with word meanings and I don't study for many tests.

Carlos

One goal for me is to plan my homework schedule better and to complete long-term projects early.

Marty

When I write essays for books or any kind of story, I want to have it the best it can be by . . . how well I write the story/essay with commas, paragraphs, quotations, etc.

Theo

Getting my average up higher by paying more attention.

Perry

My students expressed their goals in November. They had been with me for a quarter and had completed a challenging research project. They had a strong sense of what they could and could not do. They also had a feel for the kind of teacher I am, for how I present materials, and for my level of expectations. Look at how varied their needs were! Each goal was legitimately important to the student who articulated it. Trying to accommodate the variety of voices is always difficult—especially with a curriculum to cover that includes a vocabulary book, a study skills book, and some grammar. Yet this was the very first time in all my years of teaching that I had earnestly asked my students to tell me their needs. I suppose I never asked sooner because I realized that I wouldn't have all the solutions. I didn't. I reeled from the intoxication of so many expectancies and unsteadily wended my way through the rest of the year trying to address them. It wasn't easy, but I had finally asked. For me that was a big step. For the first time, I had tried to make the students the center of my concern. I attempted to create a learning community that had relevance for all involved.

After that initial probe, I was more at ease. I found myself frequently addressing students and personally inquiring what I could do to help them. I didn't have all the answers, but I learned to improvise along the way. Most important, my students came to feel my genuine concern for them.

I have to admit that I have not been immensely successful in addressing many of my students' concerns. For example, I still have not found a good way to really teach that required vocabulary book. I know that I don't spend a great deal of time with it. And even when I do, I am not sure if the students are making enough connections between the list of sixty words introduced each quarter and their current pieces of writing.

I also know that I should give more guidance to students who need help budgeting their time for long-range projects. Although I suggest that they use a calendar to distribute work equally each night, I do not always sit down with them to review their projected timetables, make suggestions, and touch bases to make sure that students are keeping up with their schedules. I acknowledge a lack of follow-through on my part. Yet I am satisfied for having attempted the task. In the future, I'll know better and do a more thorough job.

There are also goals that should have emerged but didn't. No one mentioned trying to improve comprehension skills, but as we plodded through our first piece of literature, I sensed problems. I tried literature logs. I asked students to write down their reactions to what they read, questions they had, and parts they liked or disliked; make predictions; list troublesome vocabulary; or log some of the insights they gained as they were reading. The logs were mainly done at home. Because I didn't really model the process with them, the logs did not help my students as they should have. This year, I need to do a better job teaching how to write and use literature logs. In addition, I will seek advice from successful users of literature logs.

Change begets change. There can be no stagnancy. I veer, shift, swerve, and create my own path. I come to understand that achieving the perfect classroom is not what matters. Instead, it is persistence and a willingness to make changes (even the smallest ones) that create the vital momentum behind an evolving classroom.

I Joined My Community of Learners

One of my favorite units at the beginning of the school year is to ask students to tell me about themselves as writers. I am curious to know how each individual in my class approaches the planning, editing, and completion of a written text. Last year, I decided to join my community of learners and write a language story (Harste, Woodward, and Burke 1984) of my own. Instead of writing an essay, I asked each student to pose a question that I would answer. What were my students curious about? Would they want to know what I read that influences my writing? Would they like to know my personal habits, such as prefering to write a first draft in pencil on lined paper? Would they want to know how I became interested in teaching writing? The floor would be wide open. I hoped that the activity would introduce me to my students as a learner. I also hoped that their questions would help me to really do some hard thinking about my own beliefs and abilities.

After each student handed me a question, I composed an answer and returned it. I told them that later I would compile the answers and put together a little booklet. I asked them to illustrate the questions and responses. Overall I was pleased with the questions asked and the way the answers were illustrated . . . until I happened upon one particular page. The question was, "Are you a strict grader?" My answer:

> I suppose, to be very honest, I am a strict grader. Perhaps I expect more from students in that I don't like it when they just turn in their first draft. I would like students to at least re-read their paper once or twice and really do some thinking about HOW they are expressing their ideas. I do spend a lot of time grading and I try to be as fair and thorough as possible. If you have any questions, if you want a second reading, let me know!

The illustration on the page was a sheet of student text with a noticeable *F* on it in clear, stark, red ink. This really bothered me. It showed me how some students viewed their teachers and what response they expected from teachers. I have never given an *F* grade on any piece of writing, and it is very rare for me to assign even a *D*. Yet the picture indicated that some students feel that most teachers, including myself, have very low opinions of student work. It made me very conscious of how I mark papers. How supportive am I? How destructive am I? It is so easy to mark all the errors and display dissatisfaction. It is far more difficult to point out the good because approval has always been shown simply by not applying the red pen. Yet students do not look at the clean or white areas of text to take note of what things they had done correctly. Although there is equal value in knowing what you did right as well as what you need to work on, students immediately focus upon the red marks and see only what they did wrong.

After that encounter with this student's perception, I tried to remember that many students have a very difficult time expressing themselves in writing—it is a tough task! Throughout the year I tried to preface my grades and comments with something positive before examining the weaknesses. But somehow the evaluation process still is not satisfactory, at least not to me. There must be something else I can do, but until I find it, that glaring red *F* haunts me. I have a reputation to set straight!

A Good Lesson for Me

There were two of them. Boys. As different in appearance as in interests. One young man was tall, slender, Caucasian, and possessed a passion for the author Michael Crichton. The other was black-haired and Asian, with a face that lit up at the word *Aliens.* They both had one thing in common: the boldness to approach their teacher with the suggestion that *she* do some reading! First, in a little note, my tall friend suggested that I pick up a book by his favorite author. He felt that I would enjoy it. And thus I was introduced to the world of dinosaurs and the best-seller *Jurassic Park.* The young man was absolutely right. I loved the book and devoured it soon after my return from Christmas break. But what really fascinated me was the reading level of that novel—the vocabulary and some of the concepts were quite surprisingly sophisticated. I was immediately impressed by the reading level of my student and never again looked at him in quite the same way. I *knew* what he was capable of comprehending, and all year his sparks of wit, intelligence, and insight did not escape me. This was important because he was not always a well-prepared student. He'd miss deadlines and could seem to be a pretty average performer. But he wasn't. I may never have known his true potential if I hadn't picked up the book by his favorite author.

Inspired by his classmate, the second young man invited me to share in the enjoyment of his prize possessions: comics from his collection of *Aliens*. How could I refuse? I read them and suddenly found myself conversing with my young friend in the mornings before class. It had been years since I had indulged in childhood afternoons on my back porch lost in the world of Superman, Fantastic Four, or Green Lantern. I picked up my first *Aliens* comic and was shocked. I, a teacher with a master's in English Literature, couldn't read it! What a struggle I had to get to the final page. It took me almost half the book before I could latch onto some sort of meaning, and this was only possible because I had caught the tail end of an *Aliens* rerun on television. There were so many subplots simultaneously going on. Characters flashed in and out without any context to place them. The framed action and the technical computer language overwhelmed me. I found myself both fascinated and frustrated. I read another comic. I still had problems.

The next day I met with my student and asked him many questions. I had to discuss those comics. I was determined to grasp what I didn't understand. He was quite patient with me, and we talked. He was joyously engaged in conversation that was meaningful to him and felt excited that he, a student, could guide me, the teacher. He was on equal terms. Further, my Michael Crichton fan, hearing of my plight, made me a gift of three of *his* favorite comics and asked me to try reading them. They were all number-one issues of three different series. I read them and partly understood one of the comics; the other two eluded me.

The experience of reading comic books was a good lesson for me. First, I realized that you really have to know how to approach the reading of a comic in order to be successful. There is a definite technique involved and your mind has to make leaps across galactic plots and sort out the flood of dynamic characters. To keep track of it all takes practice. But it also occurred to me that the students in my class who are not the best performers in reading comprehension are able to read comics. They have acquired the tools necessary to unlock those colorful pages, yet they cannot open the door to understanding a novel. Somehow, the keys are different, or the key hole has been repositioned so that the students can't match the hole with the key. After that experience, I wanted to discover how to make the key work.

Further, because I could not read those comics, I began to appreciate the tremendous frustrations of some of my students who cannot successfully complete the traditional literature assignment: "Read a chapter tonight and do the questions at the end for homework. Quiz tomorrow." Students do read the chapter, but they just can't pass that quiz. (I couldn't pass a test on *Pitt* or *WildC.A. T.S* and I read them— I swear I did!)

Then there was my gratitude for the concerned student who was so willing to accommodate my question asking. Those discussions were immensely important and satisfying. I began to ask myself, how accommodating am I with classroom discussions either in small group or involving the entire class? What tremendous lessons these boys taught me about the teaching of literature! How much more can I learn from my students if I just let them teach me?

In the meantime, the rest of my class was quite intrigued with the idea of *the teacher* reading materials that they enjoyed. No one ventured forth with any other favorites, but somehow just the fact that they knew I was open to all literature and respected what they liked lessened the gap between them and me.

I realize that I cannot throw my entire teaching routine out the window all at once and once and for all. I am not that confident a person. But I am content to pursue smaller avenues that will eventually lead me to the greater highways of change. The experience I shared with my two young friends sparked a possibility for this school year. Why not build a permanent classroom library (even if it must be portable) with books that *students* have chosen? I will purchase books that they recommend to me as "good reads." I will trust their judgment and ability to make choices of good literary quality. When I had a permanent room with a class library, I was the one who decided what books filled the shelves. But why can't students be recognized as being equally capable of making recommendations to their peers and to their teacher? I will begin my school year asking students for books that they'd like me to purchase, along with choices of my own. If a classroom library is for student use, then they should have some say as to what it is composed of (Rief 1992).

I'm Ready for Them

My students pass notes: "Are you going to the mall after school today?" There are quarrels between students who don't quite get along: "So and so is such a snob!" There are spats caused by the breaking of relationships: "I just hate him! He's gross!" There are romantic glances between newfound love. It's a new seventh-grade class with enough social intrigue to test the patience of a saint. But I am ready for them this year. I don't fear change. Instead, I have found myself steadfast in my belief that change must occur. I have made it a personal goal that each year I will do something a little bit different. I have made adjustments. I am armed with the knowledge that I have learned something valuable in my quest for improvement. My teaching is not the same as it was a year ago, or twenty years ago. Evolution has brought me hope.

Bibliography

Crichton, M. 1990. *Jurassic Park*. New York: Ballantine Books.

Harste, J., Woodward, V., and Burke, C. 1984. *Language Stories and Literacy Lessons*. Portsmouth, NH: Heinemann.

Keown, D. 1993. *Pitt*. Westlake Village, CA: Image.

Lee, J. 1992. *WildC.A.T.S: Covert-Action Teams*. Westlake Village, CA: Image.

Newman, J. 1991. *Interwoven Conversations: Learning and Teaching Through Critical Reflection*. Portsmouth, NH: Heinemann.

Rief, L. 1992. *Seeking Diversity: Language Arts with Adolescents*. Portsmouth, NH: Heinemann.

Verheiden, M. and Nelson, M. A. 1992. *Aliens: Book One*. Milwaukie, OR: Dark Horse Comics Inc.

Contributors

Margo Ackerman has been a Special Education teacher of elementary and middle school students in the School District of Philadelphia for eighteen years. She is currently the Educational Program Coordinator and teaches eighth-grade English at Harding Middle School. Margo's interest in making connections with people concerned about the issues of education and her desire to make school a meaningful place for all children led to her becoming a teacher-consultant with the Philadelphia Writing Project as well as a participant and site coordinator in the Urban Sites Writing Network. Margo brings to her work the voices of the many children she has taught throughout the years and those thoughts, questions, and insights of her daughters, Lindsay and Natasha.

Janet Allen currently teaches English Education at the University of Central Florida in Orlando. Prior to this, she taught English and reading at a high school in northern Maine for twenty years. In 1991, she received the Milken Foundation's National Educator Award for her literacy work with at-risk students. Her book, *It's Never Too Late: Leading Adolescents to Life-long Literacy,* was published by Heinemann in 1995.

Deborah Banks teaches grade six in Sutton, Quebec, Canada. She recently attended the UNH Writing Program, which inspired her reminiscences about teaching in the Arctic. In her spare time she reads madly, sings, writes poetry, and shares books with anyone who loves to read.

Judy Bebelaar is a published poet and a San Francisco public school teacher. She has taught English and creative writing for twenty-seven years, at a continuation high school, two public alternative schools which she helped design, and, currently, at International Studies Academy, a public charter school. In partnership with California Poets in the Schools and poet Katharine Harer, since 1984 she has produced the Galileo multicultural calendar, *And Still It Moves,* and, most recently, ISA's *We the Peoples,* and many books of student poetry. She is a Bay Area Writing Project teacher-consultant and has presented numerous workshops on writing. She has worked with local writers since she began teaching and believes bringing people who love words into the classroom is an extremely effective way to reach young people and tap their talents.

Gerardine Cannon teaches reading to ESL students at Jenks Junior High School in Pawtucket, Rhode Island, where she is also an instructor in the Multicultural Gifted Program. She is a fellow of the Rhode Island Consortium on Writing (National Writing Project), a member of the Rhode Island Department of Education Eighth-Grade Writing Assessment Committee, and a degree candidate in the joint Ph.D. in Education program at the University of Rhode Island and Rhode Island College. The mother of two daughters, Gerra Cannon Harrigan and Kate Cannon Harrigan, Ms. Cannon can be found scouring yard sales for adolescent-proof rocking chairs in her spare time.

Janine Chappell Carr has taught primary children in Oregon and now teaches first- and second-grade children at Bobier Elementary School in Vista, California. She is currently working on a book that involves a "layering of voices," as she teaches, observes, listens to, learns, converses, and reflects with the young children in her classroom.

Nick D'Alessandro has worked for the New York City Board of Education for twenty-five years as a teacher, staff developer, and—currently—school director. He is a teacher-consultant for the New York City Writing Project and began this article while teaching an I-Search course. His writing has appeared in *Pathways: A Forum for Progressive Educators, The Newsletter of the New York City Writing Project,* and *QTL: Queer Teaching and Learning.* He lives in Brooklyn.

Kyle E. Gonzalez currently teaches at Lakeview Middle School in Orlando, Florida, where she works with at-risk young adults. She piloted a Literacy Project class last year and continues to promote literacy in her work with students and teachers in Orange County. She is pursuing her master's degree in English Education at the University of Central Florida.

Judith A. Gosbee has been teaching English at Haverhill High School in Haverhill, Massachusetts, since 1969. For the past four years she has also taught the journalism course she created after being the newspaper advisor for over a decade. Since 1988, she has spent time each summer taking writing classes at UNH, where she holds two master's degrees. Judith enjoys presenting at local and state conferences. In 1990 *English Journal* published her short play, *Circular File,* based on her experiences at the New Hampshire Writing Program.

Bruce Greene has taught English and social science at El Cerrito High School for the past twenty-four years. He is a teacher-consultant with the Bay Area Writing Project and is currently active in its teacher-researcher program. When not in the classroom, he divides his time between his twin passions of fly-fishing and thoroughbred horses. Bruce is a frequent contributor to the magazine *The Bloodhorse.*

Patricia M. Gulitti, the youngest of five children, was born and raised in Port Washington, New York. Her childhood love of writing and reading were further cultivated at Binghampton University, where she received a Bachelor of Arts degree in English and General Literature. An Adelphi University internship placed Patricia in a high school setting. There she discovered her love of teaching English and learning from adolescents. Today Patricia teaches ninth-grade English in the Bellmore-Merrick Central High School district. She writes interdisciplinary curricula, advises yearbook and newspaper clubs, and in her free time enjoys listening to music, taking long walks, playing the flute, and writing.

Judy Heyboer is a bilingual teacher at Ohlone Elementary School in Watsonville, California. She is currently teaching third grade. As a member of the Central California Writing Project, she helped create a biweekly teachers' column for the *Santa Cruz Sentinel.*

Jane A. Kearns coordinates the preschool through grade twelve writing process program in the Manchester, New Hampshire public school system. A junior/senior high school teacher for twenty years, she taught for nine summers in the New Hampshire Writing Program. Now she saves summers for reading mysteries, studying waves, and traveling the blue highways of New England and Ireland.

Mary Mercer Krogness, a K–8 classroom teacher for nearly thirty years in both urban and suburban schools, has authored *Just Teach Me, Mrs. K: Talking, Reading, and Writing with Resistant Adolescent Learners* (Heinemann, 1995). Mary has also authored a commercial language arts textbook and numerous articles in *Language Arts, English Journal,* and other educational journals. She is the editor of "Middle Ground," a new column in *EJ*. She also wrote and produced *Tyger, Tyger Burning Bright,* an award-winning television series for PBS. She was invited to attend the English Coalition Conference in 1987 and the IFTE conference in 1995 and serves as a consultant to school districts. Currently she is writing fiction for young adults and has completed her first young adults novel.

Maxene Kupperman-Guiñals works as an intervenor for the Peer Intervention Program in the New York City public schools. She has been a middle school and high school teacher of English, social studies, art, drama, Spanish, and even business math for more than twenty-five years. She is a consultant for the New York City Writing Project. She has written and published articles, essays, and short stories, and served as editor-in-chief of *Teachers Not Making the Grade? A Peer Assistance Program That Works* (Peer Intervention Program 1995).

Anne G. Landis is a primary learning support teacher of emergent writers at Quakertown Elementary School, Quakertown, Pennsylvania. She received her BA at Brown University and her MEd at Lehigh University and has taught for the past twenty years. She is a novice poet.

Mike McCormick has worked as an educator in Alaska since 1976. He is the president of a concert promotion corporation, the principal of Chugiak Elementary School in the Anchorage School District, and the author of two poetry chapbooks, *Blues Before Sunset* and *Infant Poems.*

Robert Roth teaches seventh- and eighth-grade social studies at a middle school in San Francisco. He is a teacher-consultant with the Bay Area Writing Project and is an active member of its teacher research group.

Fran Wong teaches two seventh-grade English classes and four classes of eighth-grade Writing Workshop at Maryknoll Schools in Honolulu, Hawaii. She has taught junior high school students for all twenty years of her teaching career and can't imagine teaching any other age group. She is a teacher-consultant for the Hawaii Writing Project. Her love of reading, writing, and sewing has prompted her to combine all three in the production of student-made Literary Book Quilts, currently on display at the Hawaii State Library.